The 4 Faces of Frustration

How to Turn Frustration into Delight

How to Turn Frustration into Delight

Andrew Oxley

BOOKLOGIX®
Alpharetta, Georgia

BOOKLOGIX®
Alpharetta, Georgia

The 4 Faces of Frustration is a registered trademark of Andrew Oxley.

Paperback Edition November 2013

ISBN: 978-1-61005-435-5

10 9 8 7 6 5 4 3 2   1 1 0 5 1 3

Printed in the United States of America

∞This paper meets the requirements of ANSI/NISO Z39.48-1992 (Permanence of Paper)

Natalie, Drew, Ella, and Adam:

I am so very proud of you and blessed to be your dad.

To my wife, Traci:

Thank you for the incredible amount of love and support you have provided me and for reminding me what life is really all about.

"You can map out a fight plan or a life plan. But when the action starts, you're down to your reflexes. That's where your roadwork shows. If you cheated on that in the dark hour of the morning, you're getting found out now under the bright lights."

— Joe Frazier, Heavyweight Boxing Champion

CONTENTS

INTRODUCTION

Should you buy this book?

Most problems we have revolve around people.

If you are a salesperson, you need to get people to buy.

If you serve customers, you need to get them to want to come back and tell their friends and family to use your product or service.

If you lead or manage a team, you need to get them to engage and perform at a high level.

If you are an educator, you need your students to internalize and understand your message.

If you are an individual contributor, you need the assistance of others to move your work product along.

If you are a parent, you need to get your children to do some things and avoid others.

If you are in a relationship, you need to express yourself in a way that builds rather than destroys.

If you do not need people to assist you in achieving your goals, then this book will not help you. Please return it to the shelf immediately.

CHAPTER ONE

Success

Jack Staff was on cloud nine. He couldn't believe the news. He sat at his desk and stared at the phone.

"When would they like me to start?" he heard himself asking.

"Now," came the reply from Jessica. Jessica was a recruiter and had been trying to place Jack in a CEO role ever since he had turned forty.

Jack thought back to the day he had turned forty. He remembered sitting down at his desk and setting some important goals that he wanted to accomplish in his professional life. The number one goal on that list had been to be appointed as a CEO by the time he was forty-five. At the time, he had been a Senior VP and knew that he still needed to gain experience in some key functional areas before he would be ready. He had spent the last five years doing exactly that. And now the moment had arrived.

CEO. It has a nice ring to it.

He snapped back to the present and realized Jessica had asked him when he thought he could start. Jack hesitated. He knew that the right thing to do was to go and sit down with his boss and let him know what he had decided. Jessica would have to wait a couple of hours for an answer.

He let Jessica know that he would be back with her shortly, hung up the phone, and dialed his wife's cell phone. Jenny answered on the third ring.

"Hey, Jack. How are you?"

Jack smiled to himself. He knew Jenny would be excited and couldn't wait to tell her the news, but he really wanted to see her expression, so he restrained himself. He told her that things were fine, just a little slow, so he wondered if she had time to meet for lunch today. They agreed on noon at the Thai restaurant close to the mall, and Jack promised not to be late—a promise that he knew he would be able to keep this time.

Now Jack turned his attention to the matter at hand: his boss. This would not be an easy meeting. He knew that Fred fully intended that he be the next CEO. In fact, Fred had spent a ton of time mentoring and advising him over the past few years. Jack knew that Fred would feel personally betrayed by his decision to leave, but he also knew that there was no plan for Fred to retire any time soon, and no guarantee that the board would take Fred's recommendation for him to be the next CEO even when he did retire.

Jack was lost in thought as he worked his way across the floor to his boss's office. As he maneuvered his way past his coworkers, he felt a sense of regret that he had not expected. Many of these people were not just coworkers, they were his friends. It dawned on him that this was going to be tougher than he thought.

As usual, Fred's door was ajar. Jack knocked softly and heard Fred ask him to come in.

"Jack," he asked, "how are you? I haven't seen you yet today."

"I'm pretty good," replied Jack. Then, before he lost his nerve, he added, "Hey, listen Fred, there's something important I need to talk to you about."

"Oh? Well let's talk," smiled Fred, walking around his desk and motioning for Jack to sit down in one of the chairs sitting opposite his desk.

As they sat down, Jack tried to figure out how to tell Fred he was leaving. He decided the direct approach was always best.

"Fred, you know that I have set a goal for myself to be a CEO one day?" he began.

Fred nodded, so he continued.

"Well, I got a call from AmeriSys today. They have selected me as their new CEO."

There, he had said it. He sat back and surveyed his friend, waiting for his reaction. What he saw on his friend's face was not what he expected. Fred was beaming from ear to ear and had jumped out of his seat.

"Really!" he practically yelled. "That's awesome."

Jack was stunned. "You're happy?" he asked, incredulous.

"Well not for us, of course," replied Fred. "But I am incredibly happy for you and Jenny!"

Jack finally broke into a smile. For the first time since he had left his office, he felt himself relax. It was all going to be okay after all.

The Pin

The last week had been a whirlwind for Jack. He could not have asked for a more gracious soon-to-be ex-boss than Fred. Fred had made the transition out of his old job virtually painless.

Now, Jack stood in front of AmeriSys, about to enter its doors as the newly minted CEO for the first time.

Jenny had made sure he was dressed perfectly so that he made a strong first impression on the leadership team. The chairman of the board, Gary, had insisted that he meet with Jack at seven thirty for an hour and a half before he introduced him to the leadership team. After that, there would be a general session with the entire headquarters staff at noon. Jack could hardly contain himself as he strode toward the front door.

Inside, Gary was chatting casually with the janitor. There did not seem to be anyone else there yet, and in fact, Jack had been struck by the conspicuous lack of cars in the parking lot. It wasn't that he expected everyone to be there that early, but he had expected some of the senior team to arrive before him.

Gary heard him approaching and looked up with a broad smile.

"Jack, let me introduce you to Sam." Jack shook hands with Sam as Gary explained that Sam had been on staff since the very beginning, and it was rumored that he knew more of what went on around the place than anyone.

Gary and Sam shared a laugh, and then Gary looked at Jack and said, "Well, let me show you to your new office."

The office was everything Jack had expected. It was in the southwest corner of the building with an expansive view of the river. It was breathtaking. The desk was as elaborate as anything he had ever seen, as was the credenza. A boardroom-style table sat at the other end of the room with ten expensive chairs. Jack estimated that each chair was worth more than his first car.

Noticing Jack's reaction, Gary said, "Pretty nice stuff, wouldn't you say?"

Jack turned to him and just smiled. Gary sat down and motioned for Jack to do the same. He was silent for a few moments, and Jack began to wonder if he was supposed to lead this initial conversation. After a few moments, Gary spoke.

"Jack, I wanted to meet you here before all the other staff arrives so that I can give you the 'lay of the land' so to speak. The board didn't want to give you too much information before you started. I thought that was a big mistake, but I was outvoted."

Jack leaned back. He knew from the research he had done before he had interviewed that AmeriSys was not firing on all cylinders. He had assumed that was why the board had decided to fire the CEO, to sort of shake things up and get things back on the right track. His suspicions had been confirmed by every member of the board that he had spoken to.

Gary leaned forward. Apparently there was more that Gary needed to tell him.

"I know you are aware that AmeriSys has had its share of challenges, and that the board decided to make a change in the CEO. But there is more to the story. You see all this," he waved his hand indicating the way the executive office was decorated. "It's an example of all that has been wrong about the way this company has been run for the past three years. The previous CEO thought that the way to be a CEO was to dress and decorate like one. His work ethic was not great, and he created a culture that has taken a previously great company and made it, well, just plain mediocre. In fact, in many key areas, we just aren't making the grade. The board felt that they needed a fresh approach, and I convinced them that approach was you."

Jack sat there trying to take all of this in. What was Gary trying to tell him?

Gary sighed. "I don't know how to say this any plainer. AmeriSys has lost money the last eight quarters, and those losses have accelerated over the past six. If we can't reverse these losses in the next twelve months, then the board will have no choice but to sell the company."

Jack felt like Gary had taken a nice, shiny pin to the rosy, fat balloon of his dreams and popped them, all within a few minutes of entering his new office. Coming out of the haze, he noticed that Gary was still talking.

"Jack, it's not all gloom and doom. There are some good team members on your leadership team, and we still have some exceptional products and services. It's just that the service that we have been supplying to our customers has eroded over the past few years to the point that we can't bring in new clients fast enough to replace the ones we are losing. Our churn is staggering."

Jack nodded. Surely there was some good news coming next. But Gary wasn't finished. He continued, "All this has created a rather sour mood here. The employees seem to spend more time blaming each other for shortcomings than they do trying to solve the problems that exist. Even the leadership team doesn't seem immune to this sort of thinking." Gary wrinkled his brow. "It's all so alien to me," he said. "Things weren't like this when I was in charge."

He paused and looked up at Jack, who was staring out the window. Gary waited for Jack to bring his focus back into the room.

"Look, I know that the challenge is probably larger than you thought it was. However, I wouldn't have convinced the board to hire you if I did not believe you were the right person for the job."

Jack smiled back at him. *What have I gotten myself into?* he thought as Gary continued to explain the inner workings of AmeriSys.

CHAPTER TWO

Start

Jack Staff was never one to shirk from a challenge. So the news of just how close the company was to the edge of the abyss, while shocking, did not dampen his spirits for long.

Gary had arranged that the senior leadership team meet with the two of them at nine in Jack's new office. Gary's plan was to complete some introductions and then leave Jack to get acquainted with the team.

Jack had already questioned Gary about who on the leadership team was committed to fixing the company, but Gary had insisted that he wanted Jack to make up his own mind and not be tainted by his opinion. "Besides," he said, "I don't see these people often enough—I could be wrong about them." Jack sensed that Gary did not think he was wrong, but grudgingly respected Gary for wanting to be as fair as possible to the team.

The team filed in slowly; Sally from administration arrived just before nine, Bob from IT arrived shortly after nine, and John from customer service arrived about five minutes later. Carl from sales came rushing in offering a quasi-apology at about nine fifteen.

The staggered arrival allowed Jack time to introduce himself to the team individually; however, he was once again struck by the nonchalant attitude of the leadership team. Apparently, few of them thought that being on time to your first meeting with your new boss and the chairman of the board was a big deal.

As everyone settled into their chairs, Gary stood and welcomed them all. He gave a brief history of Jack's work and personal background, and then expressed the belief that, although the challenges facing the company were not insignificant, he felt that Jack and the leadership team were well positioned to make the necessary changes to help the business reach its full potential.

As Gary spoke, Jack watched the members of the team. Some were paying attention, but others were busy checking their BlackBerrys.

Gary finished up his short pep talk and let everyone know that he needed to excuse himself as he had another meeting to attend. He stood up and shook Jack's hand and let himself out the door.

Jack remained standing for a few moments and let the silence hang there. He looked around the room and smiled at his team. A few of them smiled back but not everyone.

"I know that the departure of the last CEO was a bit of a shock to you all," he began. From their reaction, he concluded that it may not have been that big of a shock at all. "I am very excited to spend some time with each of you individually, and I look forward to meeting with you over the next week. In preparation for our one-on-one meetings, I would like you to think about your functional area in terms of strengths, opportunities, challenges, and frustrations."

Jack let everyone know that they could come to him at any time and that he wanted to make sure they felt they could discuss any challenges that may occur with him.

Gauging the meeting a mild success, Jack let everyone know that they would meet again on Monday.

As everyone shuffled out of the room, Jack had a sense that the next week was going to be anything but boring. Little did he know the amount of drama that was in store for him.

Panic

At noon, Jack stood in front of the staff that worked at headquarters. He gave a passionate speech about the history of AmeriSys and how happy he was to be working with them. He was shocked that he actually could see people rolling their eyes when he let them know that he wanted their input on how they, as a team, could improve the company.

As he surveyed the people in the room, he was struck by the total lack of energy. Most people were genuinely disinterested in what he had to say. In fact, they seemed completely bored. He wondered if it was always like this at AmeriSys. Was he kidding himself that he was an engaging speaker? Was this the normal reaction when a new person took the helm at an existing company?

What had he gotten himself into?

His last company had been a positive place to work, and employees had always seemed willing to put forth the extra effort to ensure that the company, and by extension themselves, did well. He had always taken that environment for granted. But now he realized that not every company operated with that level of employee engagement.

He needed to get to the bottom of what was happening at AmeriSys, and he hoped his one-on-one meetings with his staff would shed some light on what the challenge was.

Sales

Jack had laid out a plan to speak with one of his direct reports each day, with Friday left free so that he could prepare for his meeting with them the following Monday.

His first meeting was with Carl from sales, and it was due to start in just a few minutes. Jack had spent most of the morning with the administrative details of starting a new position and trying to get up to speed on what was happening in Carl's sales and marketing group.

From what he could tell, Carl had an experienced group of sales professionals working for him. They averaged over seven years in the business, with the shortest tenure being four years. However, performance in the sales group had slipped over the past three years. Jack had learned years ago to look for the key performance indicators, or KPI for short, that would measure the success of any department. From what he could see, all the KPI in sales were not just headed in the wrong direction, they were accelerating. Carl's team was headed off the cliff, and it looked like they were intent on stepping on the accelerator all the way there!

Jack glanced at his watch. Carl was now fifteen minutes late. Just as Jack thought perhaps he had forgotten about the meeting, there was a knock at the door. Carl rushed in, full of smiles and excuses—just as he had at the morning meeting. It was déjà vu all over again, as Yogi Berra used to say.

Jack came out from behind his desk and sat down with Carl at the conference table, and Jack was once again struck by how huge the table was.

Jack spent some time asking Carl about his interests and his family, and Carl really opened up and shared a lot of information that helped Jack understand what kind of person he was outside of work. Carl was a warm and open individual, and Jack realized Carl would be a natural salesperson. People would warm to him quickly, and he was extremely likeable.

After some time, Jack steered the conversation to the areas that he had requested they consider as they prepared for the meeting: strengths, opportunities, challenges, and frustrations. Jack noted that Carl did not have any notes with him and wondered how much preparation Carl had done.

Whether he had prepared for the meeting or not, Carl dove into the conversation immediately. As Carl spoke, Jack made notes to summarize his thoughts:

Strengths:

- Experienced and skilled salespeople

- Strong relationships with customers

- Great at adapting to whatever situation arises—we get it done!

Opportunities:

- Close more sales

Challenges and Frustrations:

- Customers are not happy with customer service and not as likely to refer to us new business as a result

- Customers are not renewing their annual contracts, so we are having to find new customers to replace the ones we are losing

- The economy

After Carl finished his list, Jack went over his notes with him to make sure he had not missed anything.

Carl nodded emphatically and let Jack know that he had it exactly right.

"Is there anything you want to add?" asked Jack.

"Nope. And you know, as I sit and think about it, I think we've just been in a bit of a slump. I'm sure that once the economy improves that most of our problems will go away."

Carl smiled, and Jack had to admit that if it hadn't been for the chairman's warning that they had twelve months to fix the company, he might have believed Carl. In fact, he wanted to believe Carl!

And therein, he realized, was at least part of the problem.

Customer Service

It was Tuesday before most of the customers of AmeriSys knew that there was a new CEO on board. Jack realized this at about nine a.m., as his carefully planned preparation for his meeting with John from customer service was interrupted by the ringing of his line.

What followed was a constant barrage of customer complaints. Jack would no sooner hang up the phone than another customer would call in with a new complaint. After a while, Jack realized that there was not one area of the company that was not generating customer complaints. There were complaints about errors in billing, rude or disinterested customer service agents, salespeople making promises that could not (or would not) be fulfilled, and to top it all off, there seemed to be a never-ending series of complaints about the software constantly crashing.

Jack heard a knock at the door and looked at his watch. He had been fielding calls for two hours. Not only had he not resolved any problems, all he had to show for his time were four sheets of notes and customer contact information.

His carefully crafted plan of preparing for the meeting with John had been blown to bits, and he had not even had time to review most of the customer service group's KPI. However, if memory served him correctly, none of them were that good—and as with sales, they were headed in the wrong direction.

"Come on in," he responded as John poked his head around the door.

He walked over and joined John at the conference table. Without thinking, he remarked, "Why the heck is this thing so big?"

John seemed to be caught off guard by the question. "I'm not sure," he replied. Then he added, "I think that the last CEO thought it looked really cool."

Jack decided to focus on the task at hand and thanked John for taking the time to help him understand what was happening from his perspective. He added that he would like to get to know him a little better as well.

Jack sat back and asked a few questions about what John's interests were outside of work. He noted that John was reserved in his responses, almost as if he was not sure if he could trust Jack at this point. Jack decided not to push the point and shared a few details about his own personal life. He carefully watched John and realized that he seemed relieved that he was not going to have to share too many personal details with his boss.

Jack forced himself to slow down as he started his discussion about the customer service group with John. Jack gradually directed the conversation to the topics that he had asked them to consider as they prepared for the meeting: strengths, opportunities, challenges, and frustrations. Jack noted that John had a few pages of notes with him and had obviously spent considerable time preparing for the meeting.

The conversation had a more deliberate and slower pace with John than it had with Carl. Jack had no difficulty having the time to take notes of the discussion items that John raised:

Strengths:

- Excellent people who work hard and want to do a great job

- Great customer service skills

Opportunities:

- Not sure

Challenges and Frustrations:

- Customers are promised things by sales that cannot be done, and customer service has to mop up the mess

- Customer service gets blamed for all the problems

- There are problems with the software that we have to try to help customers with and that overloads our people

- We have too many customers to help and wait times are too long

As John finished speaking, Jack sat back and looked at the list.

"Not a pretty sight, is it?" asked John.

"Well, no," responded Jack. Then he looked directly at John and added, "I want you to know that I will work with you to help to resolve these challenges. I'm not going to tell you that it's going to be easy—it's not. But I think that by working together we can make a lot of these problems go away."

John smiled a hopeful smile and got up to leave.

"Oh, before you go," said Jack, "I want to thank you for all the hard work you and your people put in answering the phones. I know that you don't create many of the problems, but you do bear the brunt of the customer's frustration. I want to thank you for that."

"Uh...you're welcome," responded John.

It may have been Jack's imagination, but it seemed that John left the meeting with a little more spring in his step.

IT

Wednesday morning began much as Tuesday had; the only difference was that his phone started lighting up at eight rather than nine. Today, however, Jack had a plan of how to deal with the calls. The previous CEO had hired an executive assistant, and although Jack had never had a personal assistant, he decided this was a good time to get better acquainted with her.

Jack had already had some conversations with Fran, so he called her into his office and asked for her help fielding the calls that were pouring in. Fran looked less than excited at the assignment, so he decided it would be best to explain his plan.

"Fran," he began, "How long have the calls been coming in like this?"

"Since yesterday," she replied.

Jack furrowed his brow. "I don't understand. Do you mean the previous CEO never received complaint calls?"

"Well, he did occasionally. However, he never returned the calls. He would refer any calls that came to him back to John. I guess people finally just decided to stop calling him. But when you started, I guess people hoped that you might be different."

Jack could tell from the way she said the last sentence that his plan for her taking the calls indicated that she was leaning toward thinking he was not different at all.

"Let me explain why I want you to take the calls, what I would like you to do with them, and how I plan to move forward; would that be okay?" asked Jack.

Fran nodded.

"Okay, so the way I see it is that we have a lot of challenges to deal with here. In order for me to properly address those challenges, I need to understand what they are. However, if I spend all day listening to customer complaints, I won't have any time to do anything else, will I?"

Fran nodded her agreement.

"So, if you can categorize the complaints for me, then I can start to see where we might need to start with our improvements. Of course, you could let the customers know what we are doing and that we are committed to addressing their concerns. And you and I will review what you are categorizing at the end of each day. Does that make sense?"

Fran seemed to brighten up at the idea that they were going to discuss her findings and that she was not going to forever be an answering service for customer complaints.

As Fran left the office, Jack turned his attention to the upcoming meeting with Bob from IT. Bob was responsible for both the development of the company's products and the support of the internal IT infrastructure.

From what Jack could see, there were two problems that needed to be addressed in the IT group: Number one, products were taking too long to make it to market and were always way over budget. Number two, when they made it to market, there were numerous quality issues with them.

Of course, Jack realized that he had just described nearly every IT group in the country. However, there was an accelerated case of these problems at AmeriSys. The challenges coming out of the IT group permeated everything that they did. Jack knew that there would be no easy fixes in IT. He also knew that as a software company, if they did not fix IT, nothing else would matter.

Bob arrived promptly at eleven. He and Jack sat at the conference room table and had a short conversation about families and personal interests. It wasn't that Bob seemed guarded about these areas like John had been, it was just that he seemed to be ready to move on to speaking about the matters at hand—namely, the IT group.

Jack noted that the pace of Bob's speech was a little slower, much as John's had been. However, he also noted that Bob was precise in the manner in which he answered questions.

There was no need to prompt Bob for the answers to the questions he had asked at their first meeting. Not only was Bob prepared, he had typed up his responses. He handed a typed sheet over to Jack. Jack sat back and reviewed what Bob had written:

Strengths:

- Skilled people that work hard

- Great technical skills

Opportunities:

- Need more people

Challenges and Frustrations:

- Need more people

- Unclear expectations as to what products are supposed to do

- Project parameters continually change, causing delays

- Sales pushes too hard for product release before adequate testing has been done

As he completed reading the document, he looked up at Bob.

"Is there anything you want to add?" asked Jack.

"No," replied Bob. "It's pretty much all there. We are grossly understaffed and get pushed constantly to release products that we know are not ready. That creates a need to fix problems after the product is in the field, which always takes longer. It's a vicious cycle."

Jack leaned forward in his chair and asked, "How many products do you have in development right now?"

"Four."

"Okay," answered John. "Can you get me a summary of each one, including the revenue targets, staffing, when they were originally due to launch, and when each one is projected to be ready to launch?"

Bob reached into a file and handed a bound report over to Jack.

"It's all there. I had a feeling you were going to ask for that."

Jack smiled to himself. Bob was one prepared dude.

Administration

To say that Sally was in charge of administration was actually a bit of a misnomer. Sally was actually in charge of everything that did not neatly fall into the other three functional areas. Her background was in finance, and Jack was already aware that she preferred to spend her time on the financial side of the business and saw most of her other responsibilities as distractions.

Sally also had a bit of a reputation as a steamroller. Not that she didn't get things done—in fact, from what he had heard, that was her strong suit. No, it was the carnage that she sometimes left in her wake that had gotten her the reputation of being a steamroller.

In fact, Fran, his assistant, had taken him aside earlier in the week and let him know that for the past year Sally had been practically running the place and had fully expected that the board would give her the position of CEO.

That was the kind of news that Jack could really have done without.

Jack had deliberately scheduled his meeting with Sally last for all of the above reasons. He wanted to have as much insight as he could before he met with Sally.

Jack looked out his windows and thought about what he had learned so far about AmeriSys. To say that this was a deeply troubled company was an understatement. Sally would be his last face-to-face meeting before he began formulating his plan.

At eleven a.m., there was a knock on his door. He welcomed Sally into the office, and they sat at the conference table.

As Jack sat back in his chair, he noted that Sally leaned forward and was ready to talk. They exchanged a little bit of small talk. However, Jack could see that Sally was ready to move on to business.

Before he could switch gears, Sally had moved on.

"So what do you think of the situation at AmeriSys?" asked Sally.

Jack had expected Sally to be direct and to waste no time, but the question knocked him off balance for a moment. He could tell from Sally's body language, her tone of voice, and the intensity in her gaze that the question had not been posed as a conversation starter, but as a test.

Luckily for Jack, he had been through situations like this before.

"Very interesting," began Jack. "Of course, I have only had a few days to start getting to know people and what is happening at the company," he added.

Sally hesitated for a moment. "Yes, I realize that. Perhaps I can help. I have some ideas that I think will get things headed on the right track…"

"I would love to hear all about them," interrupted Jack. "But in the interest of time, would it be alright with you if we started with your functional area? Then, if we have time, we can move on to the company as a whole. If not, we can certainly schedule some more time later to get into that conversation."

Jack could tell that was not all right with Sally. In fact, her body language indicated that she really didn't see any point at all discussing her group when the issues were clearly elsewhere. However, she nodded her approval and sat back in her chair.

"Tell me a little about what your thoughts are on the areas that I had requested you consider as you prepared for the meeting: your strengths, opportunities, challenges, and frustrations."

"Well," began Sally, "on the whole, things are running quite smoothly in finance."

"Can we include the other areas you manage in our dialogue as well?" asked Jack.

"Sure, but most of my time is spent on finance," quipped Sally.

"I realize that, but let's look at it just so we don't miss anything," responded Jack.

Sally began running through the areas he had requested information on. Although she was not working from her notes, Jack was struck by the fast pace of her speech and how confidently she presented her opinions. Jack summarized her points on his pad of paper as she went through them:

Strengths:

- Employees are tenured and capable but need a lot of direction

Opportunities:

- Need employee training so Sally can get out of the small stuff

Challenges and Frustrations:

- Customer service keeps shirking their responsibilities

- IT can't hit a timeline or budget and seems to be incapable of quality control

- Sales is full of promises and there is always a "big deal" on the horizon that never seems to happen

After Sally finished speaking, Jack went over his notes with her to make sure he had not missed anything.

"Is there anything you want to add?" asked Jack.

"Just that we seem to spin our wheels constantly," added Sally. "What we need around here is less talk and more action."

"I agree with you," Jack said. "I realize that waiting and not acting is stressful for you, but can I ask you a favor?"

Sally looked at him funny, and he could tell she wasn't used to being asked for "favors."

"I'm sure you understand that I need some time to make sure that I research what the root cause challenges are at the company. So while it is stressful for you, I'm going to ask you to be patient for some time. Don't worry; the time for action will come."

Sally looked doubtful; however, she nodded her head and remarked that she would do her best.

"And as far as your ideas for how we can get things back on track, can you send those to me so I can have some time to look at them?"

"Well, they're not really written down...," began Sally.

"Well, if you could just jot them down and send me a note with them that would be great!" Jack smiled at her. Sally did not look happy with that idea, but then Jack had not expected her to be.

As Sally left the office, Jack spent some time looking at the notes he had taken during the meeting. As he had expected, Sally's challenges and frustrations had been primarily with other functional areas. She had spent little time (if any) discussing finance and administration, despite numerous attempts to get her to focus there.

Jack knew that Sally would either end up being a huge asset to the team or a huge liability. While he was determined to ensure that it was the former, he had a nagging doubt in his mind that he just could not push away.

CHAPTER THREE

Planning

Jack had been true to his word with Fran. Every day he had sat down with her and reviewed the categories of complaints that she was receiving from the customer calls she was fielding for him.

Jack had noted that although she had been reluctant to take on the assignment of fielding these calls, she had warmed to the task as she realized that there was a purpose to what she was doing.

Every day she and Jack sat down at four and looked at the list of calls she had received. Fran had gotten quite skilled at grouping the calls into categories, and she was as surprised as Jack about how few categories there had been.

Fran also appeared to have a close relationship with most people in the company, and word had gotten out that she was fielding calls for the new CEO and trying to understand what the challenges they faced were. Jack thought that was probably good for morale. But there was another unexpected outcome that happened as well.

As they began their meeting on Thursday afternoon, Jack noted that Fran was a little withdrawn as they began to review the categories of complaints.

He had asked her what was wrong, and she told him that a number of employees had started calling her with their complaints, and she had started taking notes on those as well. There seemed to be more to the story, so Jack asked her to continue.

Fran hesitated and then blurted out that Sally had confronted her earlier in the day and demanded that she share her findings. Fran had felt helpless and more than a little scared and had handed over her notes to Sally, who had read them and stormed off in the direction of Carl's office.

Fran had heard through the grapevine that there had been quite a heated discussion in Carl's office, and that Sally had left and slammed his door on the way out. Fran was almost in tears as she recounted the story and told Jack that she was now afraid that neither Carl nor Sally would trust her in the future.

Jack sat back and took a deep breath. He knew that he had to address Sally's behavior, but he first needed to reassure Fran that he was going to protect her from any negative side effects of the task that he had assigned to her.

It took him some time, but Fran finally came around and was able to focus on the task at hand. They took another twenty minutes to discuss the employee challenges and the categories that Fran had put them in. Jack thanked Fran for all her hard work and told her that he was going to talk to Sally right away.

He asked her to continue with the categorizing of the employee and customer complaints on Friday and told her that they would talk again at four the next day.

As Fran left his office, he considered the best way to deal with Sally's behavior. Clearly it could not continue. He decided that calling Sally into his office would not create the impression on her that he desired, so he took a short walk down the hall through the sales department toward finance and administration.

As he walked, he made sure that he spoke to people in the hallway. As he approached Sally's office, he noted that everyone in the department was watching him.

He knocked on Sally's door and waited for her response. Sally continued to work at her computer, and Jack decided that she may not have heard his knock. He knocked a second time, this time a little louder.

"What is it?" asked Sally without even turning away from her computer. "I'm trying to get the financials together."

"I thought we could have a brief talk," replied Jack.

Sally turned in her seat as she heard Jack's voice. The expression on her face told Jack that she had no idea that it had been him at the door.

"Sorry, Jack. I was wrapped up in the financials, and it's hard to keep any kind of focus with the number of interruptions I get around here."

Jack waved his hand and smiled as he told Sally that it was fine, but if she had a moment, there was something he needed to ask her about.

Sally said sure and turned her chair to face Jack.

Jack decided to close her door and to sit down in the chair across from Sally's desk.

"Sally, I need to ask you about something that happened earlier today. I was going over the calls that Fran has been fielding for me, and she mentioned that you had come by and asked to see them. Can you tell me what happened?"

Sally immediately sat up straighter. "Is that what this is about? Fran should know better than to listen to the whining from the sales group. Most of the issues she had taken notes on have already been fixed."

"So it is true that you took Fran's notes from her and read them?"

"Of course," replied Sally.

"That was inappropriate," said Jack. "I know you are passionate about your work. However, I need you to respect some boundaries. Fran was documenting those complaints on direction from me. It is important that if you need something like that from Fran that you ask me. Then Fran is not put in the awkward position of feeling that she has violated a confidence. Does that make sense?"

Sally was shaking her head. "There were no confidences violated. I just don't want you to get a distorted impression of where the problems at AmeriSys really lie."

Jack stood and looked at Sally. "Sally, I trust that you will have enough confidence in me to make decisions on where problems are without being swayed by other people's opinions or a few data points. While you may not have intended to violate any confidences, that is exactly what you did. There were people's names beside those complaints, which is exactly why you knew to go directly to the sales office and have a very public confrontation—isn't that right?"

Sally looked sheepish and said, "I didn't need names to know who would do the most complaining."

"Sally, I need to know that you will not repeat this sort of behavior again." Jack looked Sally in the eye as he spoke.

Sally steadily met his gaze. "Alright, I just want you to know I never meant any harm. I just want the facts presented clearly."

"Understood," said Jack. "We will all have plenty of opportunity to present the facts as we see them. But we are going to do this the right way. Is that fair?"

Sally nodded.

Jack thanked her for her time. As he exited Sally's office, he noted that a lot of heads snapped down to their work. Jack walked back across the building and noted that the staff was starting to thin out as it was now past five.

Fran was still at her desk. He stopped and sat down near her desk and let her know that he had spoken with Sally. He let her know that Sally had committed that she would not act in such a confrontational manner in the future.

Fran looked visibly relieved, and Jack could tell that she had stayed a little late to see what would happen with the conversation between himself and Sally. Fran gathered her things as Jack slipped back into his office.

Jack sat at his desk and planned his agenda for Friday. He knew that he needed to get things moving in the right direction at AmeriSys but that he needed to start with his own leadership team.

He planned to start that process at his leadership team meeting on Monday. He would need all day Friday to plan how he was going to get them to see things from a perspective other than their own.

If they could not do that, he did not see how they would ever work together as a team to address the challenges that were sinking a previously great company.

An Unexpected Mentor

Jack left the house early Friday morning. Jenny had been up with the kids and had cast him a knowing eye as he headed out the door.

She knew that the first week had not gone as he had planned, and that Jack was feeling a lot of pressure from everyone at AmeriSys— both employees and clients—to fix the issues that were dogging the company.

A number of board members had already called, supposedly to check in and make sure that Jack did not need anything. However, Jack could tell they were fishing around to see what ideas he had and what he planned to do to right the ship.

Jack pulled into the empty parking lot at seven a.m. Well, that was not entirely true; there was one car there. Sam the janitor was already at work. Jack shook his head and wondered what it would take to get everyone as interested in doing as great a job as Sam was committed to doing.

Sam was tidying the lobby as Jack entered. Sam greeted him warmly. As Jack engaged in some small talk with him, Jack recalled Gary's fondness for Sam.

"Sam, would you mind sharing something with me?" Jack asked.

Sam smiled warmly and said sure, so Jack continued.

"Sam, I notice that you always seem to have a great attitude, you seem to want to do whatever it takes to make sure this place is always spotless, and I never see you complaining. Can you tell me why that is?"

Sam stopped sweeping and considered the question.

"Well, I decided a long time ago to make sure that I was in charge of what happened in my life. That I would not let anyone else make me feel any way I do not want to feel. I just choose to be happy, and I strive to make sure I do whatever it takes to help other people be happy. Ultimately it's their choice, of course. Why do you ask?"

Jack shifted his weight and considered what Sam had just said.

"Well," started Jack, "I'm sure you may have noticed that there are not a lot of happy people around here these days."

Sam nodded his head. "I have noticed. People are frustrated with the way things are. Of course, it didn't used to be this way. So I'm certain that it doesn't have to be. People just need to understand things from a perspective other than their own. Then maybe they would be a little less frustrated with others and focus more on what they can do differently themselves."

Jack looked at Sam. "You know, I was saying that to myself yesterday. That's exactly what we need to do. I just wish I had the answer of how to make that work."

Sam started sweeping again as he remarked, "Actually, you need four ways to make that work."

"What do you mean?" asked Jack.

"Not really my area of expertise," said Sam, nodding toward the broom.

"Are you kidding?" asked Jack. "Based on your current attitude and job performance, you may be the only expert here. Would you mind having a cup of coffee with me and explaining a little more about what you mean?"

Sam shrugged his shoulders and said sure.

"Let me finish up the lobby if that is okay with you. Don't want people arriving with the place looking shabby, now do we?"

Jack agreed and asked Sam to join him in his office when he was finished and said that he would make some coffee. As Jack made his way to his office, he considered the irony that Sam wanted to make sure the lobby looked great before he started another task. The whole place was reeling with mediocrity, bad attitudes, and poor performance.

To use Sam's description, Jack would say everything about AmeriSys was "shabby." Everything, that is, except the cleanliness of the building.

Jack decided that maybe the chairman of the board, Gary, had some purpose in introducing him to Sam.

What had he said that first morning? That Sam had been there since the beginning and that it was rumored that he knew more of what went on around AmeriSys than anyone?

Jack sat at his conference table and considered what he had observed since starting at AmeriSys.

He had four different direct reports. Perhaps, since Sam had been here so long, he could share some insight into what made them tick. Then he would know how to deal with them more effectively.

His thoughts were interrupted by a knock at his door. He had left it open, but Sam clearly did not feel comfortable just walking into the CEO's office.

"Oh, Sam, please come on in," said Jack.

Sam came in and sat with Jack at the table.

"You know, I really hate this thing," remarked Jack.

Sam nodded. "It does seem a little oversized for an office," he agreed.

"Is there anything more appropriate around here?" asked Jack.

"Sure. We have a small round table that would work just as well in storage. In fact, I think it was the one that was in here originally."

"I would really appreciate it if you could switch these out," said Jack.

"What would you like me to do with this one?" asked Sam.

"Let's sell it," decided Jack. "And the chairs, too. Now, can you tell me what you meant when you said that we needed four plans to get people to look at things from another person's perspective?" asked Jack.

Sam nodded. "Well, I have found there are really four different perspectives when it comes to the way people look at things. I am sure there is a lot more to people than that, but I have found that by keeping things simple, I can understand people a whole lot faster."

"Tell me more," prompted Jack.

Sam was warming to the conversation now. "Well, I think of the four perspectives as the four faces of frustration."

"What do you mean?" asked Jack.

"Well, when people get stressed out and things are not going the way they would like, they tend to get frustrated, and when they do, that frustration shows up very differently based on which of the four they are."

"You mean like when people are stressed out because of missed deadlines, low quality, customer complaints, billing errors, and that sort of thing?" asked Jack, smiling.

Sam gave Jack a knowing glance and said, "Yeah, sort of like that."

"Tell me about the four faces of frustration," prompted Jack.

"Well, I call them the four faces of frustration because people are easiest to recognize when they are under stress or frustrated," began Sam.

Sam hesitated, looking unsure of himself.

"Go on," prompted Jack.

"You sure?" asked Sam. "I mean, it's just the way I recognize what people want from me when I am cleaning their offices. It may not really translate into anything you are doing."

"I have a feeling it will," remarked Jack. "Please tell me more."

Sam leaned back and said, "Okay. Where to start? Let's start with the one that is probably easiest to recognize."

"Which face is that?" asked Jack.

"Anger," said Sam.

"You mean they are angry all the time?" asked Jack.

"No, no, no," jumped in Sam. "Actually, quite often they are not angry at all. They just come across that way to others. They actually are just interested in getting results, and when they can't seem to get results fast enough, they become impatient, and they can appear angry to others because they are so direct."

"So what do you call people who wear the 'angry' face?" asked Jack. "You can't just call them angry people. Can you?"

"Oh, no. I try to line up a color with the way they look when they are frustrated. What color do you think I use for people who appear angry when they are frustrated?" asked Sam.

Jack thought about that. "Red?" he guessed.

"Bingo," responded Sam.

Jack sat back and thought about his direct report group. "Do you know everyone that works directly for me?" he asked Sam.

"Sure," Sam responded with a knowing smile.

"Is Sally a red?"

"How does she respond when things aren't moving fast enough for her?" asked Sam.

"She becomes frustrated and scares the heck out of others," Jack responded, thinking of the incident with Fran.

Sam nodded. "If Sally happens to be there when I clean her office, I make sure I am fast and hit the high points for her. I think of her as red."

"Okay," nodded Jack. "What's the next face?"

"The next face of frustration is the optimist. When the optimist becomes stressed, they try to see the best in everything."

"Wouldn't that be a good thing?" asked Jack.

"I thought you might say that," responded Sam.

"Why...are you saying that's me?"

Sam pursed his lips thoughtfully. "Not positive at this point. I haven't seen you that frustrated yet. But I think so."

Jack smiled.

"But to answer your question: it's not a bad thing. But neither is wanting to get things done, is it? The key is to recognize when your natural reaction to frustration is not getting you what you really want and choosing a different response."

"Tell me more about the optimists," said Jack.

"Well, they are also interested in getting results, but they tend to be more interested in engaging people to help them get things done. They tend to talk a lot and be likeable."

"What do you call them?" asked Jack

"What color reminds you of optimism?" asked Sam.

Jack thought for a moment and then answered, "Yellow, of course. And who on my direct staff fits that description?" asked Jack somewhat rhetorically.

Sam grinned as Jack wrote Carl's name down beside the yellow column.

"So far, we have the reds and the yellows. Who is next?" asked Jack.

"Next we have the face that responds to frustration by becoming fearful."

"You mean they're scared?"

"No," said Sam. "They just see problems before many of us do, especially the yellows."

"Because we are so optimistic," added Jack with a smile.

"Exactly," replied Sam. "I call these people the blues, because they tend to be factual and can come across as a little cold. Because these people are interested in avoiding problems, they tend to want to be very detailed in their work and set procedures in place to ensure that they avoid the pitfalls they see."

"Hmm," said Jack. "That sounds like Bob, wouldn't you say?"

"I think so," agreed Sam.

"What's left?" asked Jack.

"Last, we have the hardest group to recognize," said Sam.

"Why is that?" asked Jack.

"Because when they become stressed, they tend to withdraw, become quieter, and appear, well, non-emotional."

"So where the reds sort of look angry, the yellow become optimistic, and the blues become fearful, this group looks unemotional?"

"That's right," responded Sam. "And that makes them hard to pinpoint sometimes."

"What color do you use for them?" asked Jack.

"Green," responded Sam.

"Why green?" asked Jack.

"Because they sort of tend to withdraw and let everyone else have their way when they are under stress. What the greens want more than anything else is for everyone to get along. They want peace and harmony."

"Sort of the opposite of a red, isn't it?" asked Jack.

"Exactly," responded Sam.

Jack thought for a moment. "John is a green, isn't he?"

"I think so," replied Sam, looking at his watch. "I really need to go."

Jack nodded thoughtfully. "What do I do with all this, Sam?"

"I find that it helps me understand people's perspectives when I deal with them. That way I can deal with them in a manner that gets the relationship off on the right foot."

And with that Sam was out the door.

CHAPTER FOUR

Game Time

On Monday morning, Jack was in his office at six thirty. In fact, he had even beaten Sam into the office.

He had spent most of Friday and all of the weekend thinking through how to get his team to see things from a perspective other than their own. He knew that if he could accomplish that, then he could get each of them to focus their talents and abilities on what needed to be improved in their own functional areas.

The problem was that even after three days of working through how to use the four faces of frustration with his team, he still wasn't sure how to make it work. Jack could not see how telling Sally everyone thought she was angry all the time would build her up and make her want to contribute more to the team.

The same was true of all the other team members. There had to be something he was missing, and it was his hope that Sam had that missing piece.

Jack could see Sam's car pull into the parking lot shortly before seven and decided to walk down, say hello, and see if Sam had any additional insight for him.

The hallways were as empty as they had been for the past week, so Jack had no difficulty locating Sam by listening to where the noise was coming from in the building. He met Sam near the back of the storage area as Sam was loading a cart with some cleaning supplies.

"Hi, Sam," Jack called from across the room, so as not to startle him.

"Jack!" he replied. "How was your weekend?"

"To be perfectly honest, it was jam-packed with work. I've been thinking a lot about what you told me Friday, and I have a question for you if that is okay."

"Shoot," said Sam. "Is it okay if we walk and talk? I need to get the lobby cleaned up before everyone starts arriving."

"No trouble," laughed Jack.

He walked alongside Sam and thought for a moment how strange it may seem to some people that he was seeking advice on how to run the company from the janitor. But Sam wasn't any normal bird, and he was willing to take help in whatever form it came in.

"Sam," he began, "I understand the concept of the four faces of frustration, but what I have been trying to get my mind around is how to introduce this to my team. I can't see them being receptive to the news that everyone thinks they are perpetually angry, or that they are so optimistic that they ignore facts."

"No, that wouldn't work well at all," agreed Sam.

"So, how do I make them understand?" queried Jack.

"Well, I don't know about you. But I am always less defensive when I figure something out myself."

"So I need to get them to figure this out on their own? How do I do that?"

They had reached the lobby, and Sam started to busy himself with his work.

"I've always heard that if you want a better answer, you have to ask a better question," replied Sam. "All you have to do is figure out what questions to ask so that your team can teach each other what they need to know. Just keep it light and fun. Humor always helps put people at ease."

Jack pondered Sam's response. "I guess I still have some work to do designing questions, then. Thanks, Sam."

With that, Jack was off to his office. Jack closed his office door and spent the next two hours thinking through the questions he would ask his team. He needed questions that would lead them to an awareness of how they were different from one another, and how they could use those differences to become a stronger team.

When the first knock came at his door, he looked up at his clock. He smiled as he realized it was shortly before nine a.m., and he already knew who it was even before he opened it.

Sally and Bob swept into the room and sat down at his new conference table. Sam had been true to his word, and before the day was out Friday, he had replaced the fancy table with a more modest one. Jack was glad it had been changed before this meeting. He felt the table was symbolic to everything they were about to embark on.

Both Sally and Bob were clearly wondering what had happened to the conference table, but it was Sally who voiced the question.

"Uh, wasn't this table a little bigger last time we were in here?"

"Yes, it was," replied Jack. "It just seemed a little oversized for us. This one seems far more appropriate for the meetings we will be having, don't you think?"

Sally and Bob both shrugged.

John arrived right at nine, and Jack waved him into the room. He stood and shook hands with John and asked him to come and join everyone.

Jack leaned out his door and asked Fran if she would please go and let Carl know that they were waiting on him.

A few minutes later, Carl trotted in, looking for all the world like he had not yet made it to his desk. Things were still a little frosty as he took a seat as far away from Sally as he could get.

Jack decided to press forward with the meeting as Carl settled into his chair.

"Thank you all for taking the time to meet today. I know that there are pressing matters that you are having to put on hold because you are at this meeting."

Jack walked over to the whiteboard and picked up a marker and wrote "Where we are NOW" on the left side of the board.

"I have spent the past week talking to all of you, as well as many of the board members, and to be perfectly honest, way too many of our customers. I say way too many, because they are not happy, and that kind of call is painful to take in large quantities."

Below "Where we are NOW," Jack wrote: "Unhappy customers."

"I don't think anyone would disagree that our customers are not happy."

He could see a number of the team members stirring in their seats.

"Now we can debate and talk about why they are unhappy all day long. But we are not going to. For now it is enough to say that they are."

Next, he wrote: "Declining revenue and renewals."

"We are also experiencing declining revenue due to the fact that our customer renewal rates are dropping. New customers are always more expensive to obtain than renewals, so this also impacts our profitability. In fact, as everyone in this room is aware, we have lost money for the past eight quarters, and those losses are accelerating."

He wrote "Not profitable" on the board.

He paused and looked at the team. "That's where we are. We may disagree about how we got here or what we need to do to fix these problems, but there should be no disagreement about where we are."

Jack looked at each of his team members in turn. He knew that they received the same reports he did. He could also see that they did not like being told they could not discuss how they got into this mess.

However, Jack had already decided that any time spent on assigning blame was a dumb game, and he was determined not to play.

"The situation that we find ourselves in is not sustainable. But here is the good news: you are an incredibly talented group of individuals. We can and will fix the situation we find ourselves in. But make no mistake, it will not be easy. Not for me, not for you, and not for the teams that report to you."

Jack sat down and let his last statement sink in.

"This is going to be a different kind of meeting than you may be used to. You see, I chose my words very carefully earlier. I said you were a talented group of individuals. But we will not solve the problems I have written on the board as a talented group of individuals. We have to work together as a team if we are to have a chance."

Before they had a chance to think that Jack was proposing a team-building kumbaya session, he continued, "I've made sure each of you have a pad of paper at your seat, as well as a pen. I want you to write down one word that describes how you feel when you read that we have unhappy customers, that we are hemorrhaging customers, and that we are losing money."

Sally and Carl began writing immediately, while Bob and John considered the question and then wrote their response.

Jack looked around the room at their papers and smiled. At the top of each piece of paper was one word. He went to the board and wrote it at the top.

Frustrated

"What I want you to realize is that even though each one of you answered that question exactly the same way, you react differently when you are frustrated. In fact, when you think about it, your teams likely react very differently from each other as well."

"Yeah," said Sally. "I try to fix problems while other people sit around and talk about them." Sally looked sideways at Carl, Bob, and John as she spoke. Her three peers looked back at her with what could only be described as contempt.

Jack stepped forward and addressed Sally. "We all react differently, Sally, and we look at other people's reactions to challenges from our own perspective. I don't dispute anyone at this table's commitment to fixing AmeriSys. But we must stop attacking each other if we are ever going to work as a team." He looked directly at Sally as he said this. He kept his tone pleasant and conversational, but made sure that Sally knew that kind of comment was not appropriate.

"As I said, we all react differently when we feel frustrated. What I want to share with you is a simple way of understanding how each of us responds."

Jack drew a horizontal line on the board. On one end he wrote "FASTER," and on the other he wrote "SLOWER."

SLOWER ◄───────────────────────► **FASTER**

"Let me ask each one of you a question. Especially when you are frustrated, do you desire to work faster or to slow down?"

Sally immediately answered "Faster," as did Carl.

Bob looked unsure and asked, "Doesn't it depend on what is happening? I mean you may have to move faster in some cases and slow down in others."

"Excellent point," said Jack. "Although we will act differently depending on what the situation is, we all have a preferred way of responding."

He looked at Bob and asked, "Bob, when you feel frustrated, would you *prefer* things speed up or that they slow down?"

"I guess if you put it that way, I would prefer they slow down so we can figure out what is happening and make sure we fix the problem and not a symptom of the problem." He glanced at Sally as he said this, but Jack decided to let it go as Sally seemed to be unaware the jab was intended for her.

John had identified "Slower" as well. Jack wrote their names on the line where they had identified themselves, so that it looked like this:

Bob, John   *Sally, Carl*
SLOWER ◄─────────────────────────► **FASTER**

"So you can see," he continued, "that there is some difference in the way that the team addresses problems and challenges. "

"Which way is right?" asked Sally.

Jack appreciated that she had not provided her opinion and had rather asked a question. He took that as a small amount of progress.

"Well, I think Bob said it best a minute ago. It really depends on the situation. We are just talking about our preferred way of operating here."

Sally did not look in the least bit convinced and sat back with a look of disbelief. Jack knew that Sally would be a great ally once she was won over, but that was not going to happen easily, so he let the point go.

He walked back to the board and drew a vertical line, perpendicular to the first line, and wrote "TASK" at the top and "PEOPLE" at the bottom, so that he had created a grid.

"Now let me explain the difference between these two. People tend to be more oriented toward one end or the other of this line, just like with the previous one. That is not to say that if you are more oriented toward tasks you do not like to be around people, it's just that sometimes it is easier to get things done, faster or the right way, when we work by ourselves. In a similar way, if you are more oriented to the people end of the line, it's not that you don't want to get things done, it's just that you like to get things done with and through people."

Jack paused to see if this was sinking in. He could see some nods, and he decided to start with Carl this time, who finally looked like he was fully engaged in the meeting.

"Carl, which end of that line do you think you are more comfortable on?"

Carl laughed. "Oh, let me see...I think I might be a people person. Like you said though, I still want to get things done. I just want to get things done with other people."

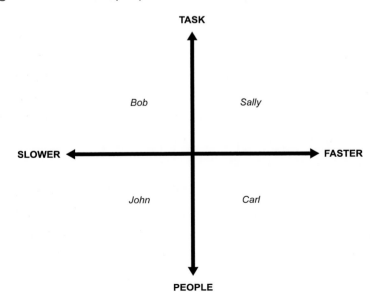

Everyone had a good laugh as Jack wrote Carl's name in the lower right-hand quadrant.

"Sally, how about you?"

"Top right." Realizing she had skipped a step in the process, Jack smiled to himself. Jack wrote her name up in the top right quadrant.

"So you would say you are more task-focused than people-focused?" asked Jack, wanting to make sure he confirmed her point of view.

"Yes," responded Sally.

Jack turned to Bob. "Where would you say you are, Bob?"

"I think I probably am more task-focused, at least that is more comfortable for me. I have learned to work with the people on my team to get things done, but that's not really the same as what I prefer. So yes, top left."

Jack wrote his name on the board in the top left quadrant.

"John, how about you?"

"Definitely more people-focused," said John. Jack wrote his name down in the lower left hand corner.

Jack stood back and looked at the board. "So let's see. Here's what we have so far: Sally's preferred work style is to work on tasks at a faster pace. Carl's preferred work style is to work at a faster pace, but with and through people. John's preferred work style is to work at a slower pace, but with and through people, and Bob's preferred work style is to work on tasks at a slower pace."

"Every one of us is different," remarked Bob.

"Yes, and it's a good thing we are, too!" added Jack. "You see, each one of your departments has a different type of work. Sally's group handles a lot of transactions and needs to move relatively quickly to make sure everything gets done. Carl's group also needs to move quickly, but needs to focus on building relationships with the clients. John's group needs to be great listeners to the clients' needs, which often requires slowing down. And Bob's group does a lot of detailed work, where quality is paramount."

Jack came and sat down with them. "So not only are you different in the way you approach your work, so are the groups you lead. And it turns out that is a good thing. But not all good. You see, those differences in work style also drive frustration when our work groups need to interact. Until we start to understand each other better, and start to respect the different ways we approach our work, we will always just be a group of talented individuals—but we will never be a team. In order to address the challenges of where we find ourselves, we must act as a team."

Jack looked around the table and let that last statement sink in. Sally was studying the board and then remarked, "So are you saying that there are times we need to change and respond differently based on what the situation requires, rather than what is comfortable for us?"

"That is exactly what I am saying. And the good news is you already do it, at least some of the time."

"But there are times when we don't, right?" asked Carl.

"Yes, there are," responded Jack.

John looked down at the pad of paper in front of him. The word "frustrated" was printed there in big letters.

"That's when we struggle with adapting, isn't it?" asked John.

"I think so," replied Jack. "Not just then, but that is when it seems the hardest. And since we are all under a lot of stress right now, we may be tending to respond in our natural style a lot."

"So what do we need to do?" asked Sally.

Jack smiled. "That's where things get interesting."

The Four Faces

"I have been giving a lot of thought to the different ways that we respond to each other, especially when we are under stress," began Jack. "I thought it would be helpful if we had some terminology to use to describe the different ways we respond, so that we start to recognize the patterns of behavior at AmeriSys. By doing this, we should be able to systematically recognize where people are coming from and understand their motives better, rather than making assumptions, and shift the way we respond. This is so that we can achieve more of what we all want—better business results. Does that sound like a plan to all of you?" he asked the team.

Everyone seemed to be in agreement, so Jack continued.

"In order to get the next part of this completed, I am going to have to ask if you will be willing to play 'all out.' What I mean by that is that I am going to ask you to give feedback to each other that will help us move forward. I am also going to ask you not to take offense to the feedback you receive."

Sally looked around the table, and her expression indicated she was dubious that her peers would avoid taking offense to feedback; however, everyone seemed to be playing along, so Jack continued.

"Now, just because someone gives you some feedback does not mean that you are that way, all it means is that you may seem that way to them, especially when you are under stress. What I am going to do is ask you to describe how one of your peers acts toward you when they are frustrated or under stress. Here is the way we are going to do this: Bob, you will be giving feedback to Carl. Carl, you will be giving feedback to Bob. Sally, you will be giving feedback to John. And John, you will be giving feedback to Sally."

Bob asked, "So I am going to be considering how Carl acts toward me when he is frustrated or stressed out, is that correct?"

"Exactly," answered Jack. "I am going to give you sixty seconds to write your thoughts down in front of you on your pad. Then we will share. Sally and Carl, I know you may not need sixty seconds, but remember our grid. John and Bob may need a little more time than you to consider their responses."

"I don't," said Bob.

"Nor I," added John.

Jack took a deep breath and realized that this could go horribly wrong. What if they did not see things the way that he did? Realizing it was too late for second guessing now, Jack decided to forge forward.

"Okay. Bob, how does Carl appear when he is under a lot of stress and is feeling frustrated?"

"That's easy," began Bob. "When Carl becomes stressed he starts assuring everybody that everything is going to be okay. He keeps saying 'Trust me' like that is supposed to be some kind of confidence booster."

"Would you say he becomes a little too optimistic, in your opinion?" asked Jack.

"Yes. More than a little," replied Bob.

"How does that make you feel?" asked Jack.

"It drives me nuts," said Bob. "When we have issues that need to be addressed, we need to dig in and solve the problems. What is that saying? Oh yeah, 'Hope is not a strategy.' But sometimes for Carl it seems to be."

Jack looked over to Carl, who was looking at Bob in disbelief. Carl started to reply, but Jack held up his hand and stopped him. "As hard as this is Carl, I want you to understand that Bob is only telling you how you appear to him when you are frustrated or stressed. That does not mean you are that way."

Jack added, "I want you to write down how you feel after receiving that feedback from Bob, but don't share it with the team right now."

Jack waited while Carl wrote a few items on his pad.

"Now," continued Jack, "I want you to think about what Bob has to say. Ask yourself this question: Is there at least some part of that feedback that may be true?"

Carl considered that for a moment and then responded, "Maybe some. I do always try to see the glass as half full. I think you have to in order to find a solution..."

"Okay," interrupted Jack. "Now, Carl...how do you see Bob when he is under a lot of stress and is feeling frustrated?"

Carl was ready with his answer and seemed primed after having to take his knocks from Bob. Of course, Jack had counted on that and had asked Bob to share first for exactly that reason.

Carl smiled and said, "Bob, I don't want you to take this the wrong way. When you become stressed, you sort of lock down. Everything seems to stop. It's like you are afraid to make a mistake, and you want to make sure that every decision is perfect."

"So would you say that Bob may slow down too much like he is afraid of making a mistake?" asked Jack.

"Exactly," said Carl.

Jack looked over at Bob, who looked like he was studying Carl as you might a specimen at the zoo. He neither spoke nor appeared to even acknowledge that Carl had been providing feedback.

"Bob, I want you to write down how you feel after receiving that feedback from Carl, but don't share it with the team right now."

Jack waited while Bob wrote some notes on his pad.

"Now," continued Jack, "I want you to consider what Carl had to say and ask yourself this question: Is there at least some part of that feedback that may be true?"

Bob nodded. "I think so. I definitely slow down when I am frustrated. I feel that I need to make sure that we don't continue to make the same mistakes."

"I see," added Jack. Jack turned back to Carl and asked, "And how does that make you feel?"

"Like he does not understand the magnitude of the problem, and all he wants to talk about is why it will not work. He just seems like a complete pessimist."

"So what does that make you want to do?" asked Jack.

Carl answered, "I try to get him to see the positive strides we are taking and assure him that it is going to be okay." A look of realization spread over Carl's face. "Which is what frustrates you, right?" he asked Bob.

Bob nodded his agreement.

Jack, realizing they had made a huge leap forward, added, "Do you see how easy it is to get into a vicious cycle if we only see things from our own perspective?"

Both Bob and Carl seemed to be on board with that premise, so Jack turned his attention to Sally and John.

"Okay, Sally. How does John appear to you when he is under a lot of stress and is frustrated?"

Sally looked a little perplexed. "I don't know," she finally said. "I can't say that I know when John is stressed or frustrated by the way he acts, it's more by what doesn't happen."

"What do you mean?" asked Jack.

"Well, I leave our meetings thinking that he has agreed to do whatever we discussed, but then it never seems to happen."

"So would you say that it is hard for you to read what is happening with John?" asked Jack.

"I would say so."

Jack instructed John, "John, I want you to write down how you feel after receiving that feedback from Sally, but don't share it with the team right now."

John made a few notes and then looked back up at Sally and Jack.

"Now," continued Jack, "I want you to consider what Sally had to say and ask yourself this question: Is there at least some part of that feedback that may be true?"

John pursed his lips and considered the question. Carl started to answer for him, but Jack raised his hand to let him know that he wanted John to answer this question.

"I think so. I feel like when Sally comes to me with a problem, she wants an immediate solution. When I try to talk with her about what happened, I feel that she does not listen to me."

"How does that make you feel?"

"Like she is not interested in solving the real problem. I feel she just wants to assign blame."

Jack nodded his head. "John, how do you see Sally when she is frustrated or stressed?" asked Jack.

John looked at his notes and appeared to be trying to decide how to respond. John took a deep breath and finally said, "Angry." He added as he looked at Sally, "You seem angry. A lot. "

Jack decided to help out. "So when Sally is frustrated, she comes across to you as angry. Whom does she seem angry with?" asked Jack.

"Everyone," answered John. "The customer, me, the staff. Everyone."

"How does that make you feel?" asked Jack.

"Like there is no point in talking to her."

"I see," added Jack, looking at Sally who was sitting in shock.

"Why is there no point in talking to her?" asked Jack.

"Because it doesn't make a difference. She doesn't listen."

"Sally, once again, I want you to understand that John is only telling you how you appear to him when you are frustrated or stressed. That does not mean you are that way. I want you to write down how you feel after receiving that feedback from John, but don't share it with the team right now."

"Now," continued Jack, "I want you to consider what he has to say and ask yourself this question: Is there at least some part of that feedback that may be true?"

Sally considered that for a moment and then responded, "I'm not angry. I am frustrated with the pace at which things happen...or actually, that they don't happen around here..."

"So," interrupted Jack, "let's see what we have so far. If it is alright with you, I am going to take some liberties with the grid we have created. I thought it might be helpful if we associated a color with each of the 'faces of frustration' we have identified. Here is what I have so far: anger – red, optimism – yellow, withdrawal – green, and fear – blue."

Jack looked through his portfolio and found the graphic that he had designed for his team and handed it out to them. Jack looked at his team. "You see, we all see the world differently. None of us sees it entirely accurately. Now. What are we going to do with that knowledge?"

The Four Faces of Frustration

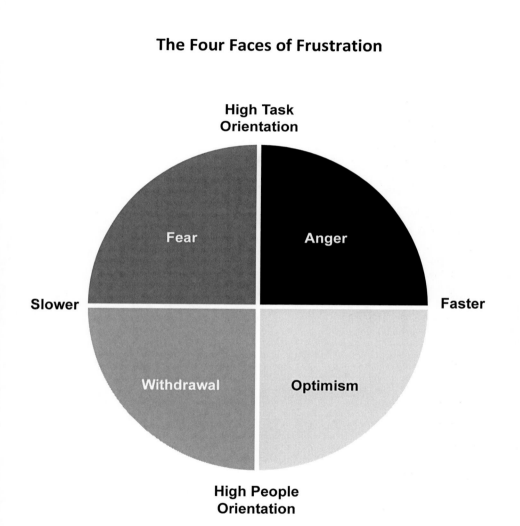

CHAPTER FIVE

Casting a Larger Net

On the following Monday morning, Jack was in his office at six thirty. He had asked his four key direct reports to take some time and consider what they had learned about each other. He had asked them to think about what some possible next steps should be and to be ready to discuss them at their meeting at nine a.m. Monday.

To his wife's great disappointment, he had spent the weekend thinking about how he should proceed. He could tell that Jenny was still excited about the new opportunity he had taken on. However, the reality of the hours he was working was definitely taking some of the edge off the excitement for her.

In fact, he had gone to a local print shop and asked them to design and print a graphical representation of what he had now started calling the "four faces of frustration." He had the poster pinned to his wall by his *new* conference table.

The Four Faces of Frustration

**High Task
Orientation**

Slower .... **Faster**

**High People
Orientation**

As the time moved closer to seven a.m., Jack almost subconsciously shifted his attention to the parking lot, watching for Sam's car to arrive. Like clockwork, he saw Sam's car pull into the parking lot at ten minutes before seven, and started his way down for his now familiar early morning meeting.

Jack called out to Sam as he was entering the building, and Sam greeted him warmly.

"Well, how did it go with your team?" asked Sam. "Did you figure out a way to get them to understand how they see the world differently?"

Jack laughed as he answered. "I think so. And you were right; all I needed to think of were the right questions."

He then asked if Sam would be willing to join him upstairs for a few minutes when he finished with his early morning duties. Sam agreed and said he would see him upstairs shortly. As Jack climbed the stairs back to his office, he realized that he had two purposes for asking Sam to come up. He certainly wanted to pick Sam's brain some more on how to use the four faces with other parts of the company. However, he was also proud of his accomplishments thus far and wanted to share those with Sam. He realized that he was gaining a deep respect for Sam and that there was a lot more to him than met the eye.

Sam arrived in Jack's office at exactly seven fifteen. Jack invited him in as he looked at his watch. He tilted his head to the side as he smiled at Sam and asked, "You're very punctual; is that because you are a blue, perhaps?"

It was Sam's turn to smile. "I can see why you would say that; however, you should be careful not to take one behavioral clue from someone and make an assumption about their behavioral style."

"Point taken," replied Jack. "But you did not answer my question."

Sam smiled coyly but said nothing.

"Okay. Never mind. But I'll figure you out yet, Sam," said Jack.

Sam's eyes drifted over to the poster. "I see you have been busy."

Jack took a few minutes to explain how he had conducted the meeting the previous Monday and how his team had responded. "I spent the week and even the weekend thinking about what to do next," admitted Jack.

Sam nodded as if considering the question but made no move to respond. After a short time, Jack decided he had better ask more directly.

"What I really need to do is get all the staff at AmeriSys thinking about this and modifying their behavior based on what is best for other employees and especially for the customer. Sam—you've been here a long time, and you have been a great help to me in the short time I have known you. Would you mind spending a few minutes brainstorming this with me?"

"Of course," replied Sam. "You do know that you're the boss, don't you?"

"I know," said Jack, "but this is way outside of your normal duties."

Sam smiled. "I'll help you any way I can."

With that, Sam and Jack launched into a discussion that would change AmeriSys forever.

Just before nine, Jack was as ready as he would ever be for his next staff meeting. This was a good thing because his team was apparently itching to get started. He found Sally, Bob, and John all waiting outside his office when he went out to say good morning to Fran. At the same time, he saw Carl practically sprinting down the hall with a big grin on his face. Everyone turned to watch his breathless arrival.

Carl slid to a stop and remarked, "I figured that since I am usually the one holding up meetings by being late, I should be a little less 'yellow' and make sure I was on time this morning."

The team shared a laugh as they walked into Jack's office and seated themselves around the conference table.

Jack took a deep breath and looked down at his plan. "Well, you have had a week and the whole weekend to think about what we discussed last week. I am interested to hear what your thoughts are and how you think we might be able to move forward in addressing the challenges we face in turning AmeriSys around."

Not surprisingly, Sally was the first to speak up.

"Look, I don't want to offend anyone, but it seems to me that what we need to get focused on is what our customers need. We have a product that is flawed in its design, our customer service people seem to be incapable of solving customer complaints, and we are losing customers in droves. We have to have more of a sense of urgency around addressing these problems! I mean, no offense, Jack, but while I appreciate you trying to get us all to play well in the sandbox together, we have got to start fixing these problems."

Sally sat back and looked at Jack. In fact, everyone was looking at Jack. Jack took a few moments to consider his response as he looked around at his team. On the one hand, he felt that Sally's outburst was a direct challenge to his authority. At the same time, he knew that he was trying to foster open dialogue at the company, and how he responded would do more to establish expectations on his team than anything he might say for the foreseeable future.

Having made his decision, Jack turned to Sally.

"Sally, I respect your passion and urgency to solve the problems we face. However, it is critical that we address these problems as a team. We need not just every person here, but every person in the company pulling together in the same direction in order to do that. Now, you may not agree with the direction I am taking, but I am going to ask you directly: can you support it?"

Jack waited and a heavy silence descended on the room.

Sally finally relented. "I can support this for now. But we have to start doing some things differently if we are going to make progress."

Jack recognized the qualifier in that statement but decided to let it pass—for now.

Jack nodded. "I realize that it may seem that we are moving slowly to you, but I assure you all that we are going to start working through the many challenges we face. In fact, we are going to start working directly on our challenges this week."

Having averted a mini coup, Jack turned his attention to the rest of the team.

"How about the rest of you? What are your thoughts about what we discussed last week and how we might be able to move forward in addressing the challenges we face in turning AmeriSys around?"

Carl was the next to speak up. "I have been thinking that many of the challenges we face in sales, both internally and with our clients, could be avoided or at least managed better if we used some of the ideas you shared."

John was nodding. "I think our customer service representatives would really benefit if they could modify their approach based on who is calling in. I think that sometimes we may use an approach that makes the situation worse with the customers."

"What do you mean?" asked Jack.

"Well, it seems that a lot of our customers are really angry when they call in. Maybe we are trying to solve their problems the way we would want a problem addressed, rather than how they would want the problem solved."

Warming up now, John continued. "For example, I think a lot of our people have more blue and green than anything else. So they tend to want to slow things down when a customer calls in order to make sure we solve the problem the right way. However, more often than not, the customer is so angry that they seem to want to just yell at us and tell us we are not moving fast enough. That stresses our people out even more. If we could find a way to make sure that they understood how to deal with customers based on what they need, I think we could have better outcomes."

John seemed to be looking around at the team for validation, and Jack noted that Carl immediately jumped to support him. "I see the same thing in sales," said Carl. "But I think it may go even deeper than just recognizing the customer's style. I think we need to understand our own natural approach, and how that may or may not be allowing us to serve the customer in the best way."

He paused and then added, "You know, that might not just impact how many sales we close, it may also impact the promises we make in the process."

Both John and Bob perked up at this point and seemed to take more interest in what Carl was saying. It was clear that the promises coming out of the sales group were a huge source of frustration for both of them. Jack allowed the group to consider John's and Carl's comments for a moment and then asked Bob for his thoughts.

Bob sat for some time and seemed to be trying to figure out how best to answer the question. Jack could see both Carl and Sally almost squirming in their seats.

After a few moments, Carl asked Bob, "Do you mind if I help out some?" Bob turned to him as Carl continued. "The way I see it…"

Jack smiled and cleared his throat. "Carl. What just happened there?"

"What do you mean?"

"Why did you feel that you needed to help Bob out?"

Carl thought for just a moment and replied, "I don't know…it just looked like Bob could use some help."

Jack turned to Bob. "Did you?"

Bob shook his head no.

Jack asked, "Bob, when you were quiet there, what was happening with you?"

"I was considering the best way to answer your question," replied Bob.

Jack nodded. "You see, both Bob and John like to process information and plan their response before they start speaking. On the other hand, Carl, you and Sally are more comfortable with quicker responses, as you are okay with speaking while you think it out."

"So when I try to 'help,' that probably doesn't come across as helpful, does it?" Carl asked Bob.

"I know you mean well," replied Bob, "but really all it does is cause me to have to then consider the original question as well as your response. It actually makes the conversation take longer."

"Or I just let you make the decision," added John. "It has always seemed that you were not really that interested in my opinion, as you almost always answered any question you asked me. I think what I am realizing now is that maybe we just process information differently and you were just trying to help."

Carl smiled. "But I wasn't helping, was I?"

Both Bob and John chuckled. "Not usually," laughed Bob.

Jack turned his attention to Bob. "Which brings us back to the original question: how do you see this working with your group?"

Bob, having had some time now to consider his response, knew exactly what to say.

"I think we may get so detail-focused that it may be difficult for us to prioritize the vast number of challenges that come our way. In addition, I wonder if the differences in our communication style may get in the way of getting a really accurate project scope outline from both Sally's and Carl's teams."

Jack nodded as he looked from Sally to Carl. Carl was also nodding, but Sally seemed less than happy with the comment from Bob. Jack decided to risk drawing her out.

"What are your thoughts on that, Sally?"

Sally looked at Jack and then addressed Bob.

"I think that he may be right. I think Bob's team does get sucked down into the weeds on details way too much. And when it comes to our R&D team outlining either a product revision or a new product, well let's just say that they seem incapable of grasping the big picture."

The expression on Bob's face had not changed one bit since Sally started her assault. However, everyone, with the possible exception of Sally, was aware that a chill had entered the room.

Jack sighed inwardly and tried to compose himself.

After a moment, he asked, "Sally, is that the way you see it?"

Sally turned in her chair to face Jack. "Yes, it is. And I know you are going to say that there is a different side to that story."

Her body language, however, did not indicate a willingness to hear another side to the story.

Jack finally said, "Let's look at this another way, Sally. Can you think of anything that you or your R&D team may do that could possibly contribute to the challenge Bob described?"

Sally considered that for a moment and responded, "Well, sometimes we may be in a rush to get a product to market, and we may not spend enough time making sure that Bob's team is totally clear on the project scope. It's just that they are so infuriating with the level of detail they get sucked down into. It's not that the detail isn't important. I know it is. I just feel that they are so focused on the trees that they lose sight of the forest."

Bob's expression still had not changed as he responded, "Like I said, a difference in communication style."

Jack nodded. "So would it be fair to say that there are probably applications to see things from another perspective in every one of your groups?"

Everyone nodded, even Sally, although considerably less energetically than the other three.

CHAPTER SIX

The System

Jack breathed a sigh of relief as his team departed. The session had been successful in so much that he felt that each individual had come to the awareness that perhaps there were things that they could change. Things that would help the organization run more effectively. But they were not yet a team.

Jack knew that a team is not just a collection of talented individuals who are willing to admit they need to get better. A team is much more than that—and AmeriSys was not even close.

Now that he had at least surface agreement from his DRG (Direct Report Group), the question was where to go next. Jack needed to address all areas of the company immediately. However, he knew that more than anything else he needed a "win." He needed proof that this approach had the ability to change the company's results in some area. The questions was: where?

Jack got up and went over to his whiteboard. In big letters at the top of the whiteboard he wrote:

Priority: Change results quickly.

He then considered the pros and cons of starting with each of the key areas of AmeriSys:

<u>Sales:</u>

- Responsible for all new revenue coming into the company

- Currently making too many promises that either cannot be kept or are expensive to keep—both in terms of time and conflicting priorities for the IT group—which increases the pressure on the customer service group and increases "churn"

- Are far too optimistic about short- and long-term sales prospects

<u>Customer Service:</u>

- Responsible for all monthly recurring revenue coming into the company

- Currently having difficulty retaining customers, putting more pressure on sales to increase sales to new customers

- Seem to have difficulty working with customers to resolve their complaints

<u>IT:</u>

- Have way too many projects underway

- Have far too many conflicting priorities

- Projects way behind schedule and way over budget

<u>R & D – Accounting – Administration:</u>

- Too little quality control

- Too many billing errors

- Systems are antiquated

- Too much control from the top

- Too little communication and consultation with IT

Jack stood and looked at the board. It was clear to him that although Sally was a pain and was fighting him at every turn, her group was not the immediate priority. He stepped back and asked himself if he was rationalizing not working with Sally first because she was so difficult.

He shook his head. No, that wasn't it. He needed a win to help convince her to buy into the system he had in mind, and that win would come faster and have a more significant impact on the bottom line if he started elsewhere.

In a similar way, IT was also not the place to start. Clearly, there were issues that needed to be addressed, but the timeline to fix those challenges was too long to allow for a quick win.

That left sales and customer service.

As Jack considered the problem of customer retention, he realized that both sales and customer service contributed to the problem. Sales made too many promises that were either expensive or impossible to keep. Customer service was cleaning up the mess that sales was creating but doing a poor job of retaining customers. How much of that was their fault was hard to figure out at this point.

Jack looked back and forth between sales and customer service. It had to be sales. That should take some of the pressure off the customer service group.

There was a risk, however. If he asked the sales team to back off making their "inappropriate" promises, sales would no doubt drop. That would cause an acceleration in the short-term losses that the company would sustain.

Jack wondered how long it would take for the board to get involved and start questioning his plan. He figured he had three months tops, perhaps less.

Jack knew that as a leader, there were no certainties. The only thing he could do was make the best possible decision based on the information available. He had to start with sales.

Now, he had to decide what to do to turn around the sales department. He knew that Carl would be receptive. He always was. The challenge was how to engage Carl in the process so that he would follow through on the commitments that he made.

Jack picked up the phone and asked Fran to arrange a mandatory sales meeting for eight the next morning. He knew there would be grumbling about the short notice; however, he also knew that the chances of anyone having to move a sales call based on the meeting were extremely low. He knew this because he had observed that few sales calls occurred until lunchtime. It was almost as if the sales team was more interested in socializing than selling. Jack then spent the rest of the day planning the way he would interact with Carl's team.

The next day, Jack arrived early, as was his custom. At eight, he strolled down to the sales department to meet and greet the team. Since their workday started at eight, he had expected that most, if not all, the team would have arrived on time for the meeting.

That would not be the last surprise he would receive that day.

As he arrived in the sales department, it appeared to be empty. Well, not exactly empty. Sam was there cleaning up a bit and generally just making sure that things were straightened up. He smiled as he saw Jack approach.

"Where is everyone?" asked Jack.

Sam looked around the office. "I think they normally get in closer to nine."

Jack looked disappointed. Sam placed a hand on his shoulder and smiled.

Jack smiled back at him and asked, "This isn't going to be easy, is it?"

Sam shook his head. "Nothing worthwhile ever is. Good luck."

And with that, he wheeled his cart back out into the main hall.

Jack decided to go ahead and set up his stuff in the conference room across the hall from the main sales area. That way he could observe and say hi to the team as they arrived.

The team started to trickle in just before nine. Jack made sure that he greeted each team member, especially Carl, who arrived almost exactly at nine. Jack made a mental note to make sure he discussed with Carl how important it was to model what you wanted from your team.

As the team settled into the conference room with coffee and donuts, Jack glanced at his watch. It was 9:20.

Jack took a deep breath and started addressing the team. As with earlier conversations, he had decided that the best way to engage them was to ask questions.

"Good morning, everyone. Today I want to talk with you about how we can radically increase not just the number of sales we are making, but also the quality of the sales we are making."

He paused and looked around the room.

"Now I know that may sound like a tall order, and actually, it is. However, I am not going to ask you to work any more hours than you are supposed to be working."

Jack had chosen his words carefully, and he noticed that a number of the team members shifted uncomfortably in their seats while others seemed unaffected.

He continued, "I am, however, going to ask you to interact with and sell to your customers differently. You see, each one of you has a preferred selling style. And not surprisingly, each of your customers has a preferred buying style. The key is to make sure that we are selling to our customers the way they want to be sold to."

Jack paused and looked around the room. Most of the group seemed attentive enough, although a number of the more seasoned members of the sales team looked like they were unsure what he, as an operations guy, was going to teach them about sales.

"What I am going to talk to you about today is a simple approach that will help you match your style to your customers. The goal of all of this is to increase sales and to make sure that we are getting the right kind of sales, so that we are not having to make promises that are either very hard or expensive to keep."

Jack saw a number of heads pop up at his last statement. *Good*, he thought. *Now I have everyone's attention.*

He went over to the whiteboard and led the team through the same exercise that he had led the executive team through.

He asked, "When it comes to selling our services, I want you to consider whether you prefer to move quickly or more slowly."

Not surprisingly, the majority of the sales team preferred to move more quickly. Jack added their names to the board as they indicated their preference.

SLOWER ◄──────────────────────► **FASTER**

Joe, Frank   *Dan, Greg, Joelle,*
                                                              Ken, Tom

Jack continued, "In addition to a preference of whether we like things to move more slowly or faster, we also have a preference about how much we want to socialize in the sales process."

Jack drew the vertical axis in, with "Task" at the top and "People" at the bottom.

"Now let me explain the difference between these two. People-oriented salespersons tend to be more relationship-focused. Task-oriented salespersons tend to be more focused on getting the job done either quickly, or making sure it is done correctly, which usually means ensuring we provide a lot of detail to the customer. That is not to say that if you are more oriented toward tasks you do not like to socialize with people, it's just that sometimes it is easier to get things done, faster or the right way, when we focus more on the task at hand. In a similar way, if you are more oriented to the people end of the line, it's not that you don't want to get things done, it's just that you tend to want to build strong relationships through getting to know the customer."

Jack spent a few minutes allowing each member of the team to determine where they thought they resided on the Task–People line and then stood back and looked at the graph they had created.

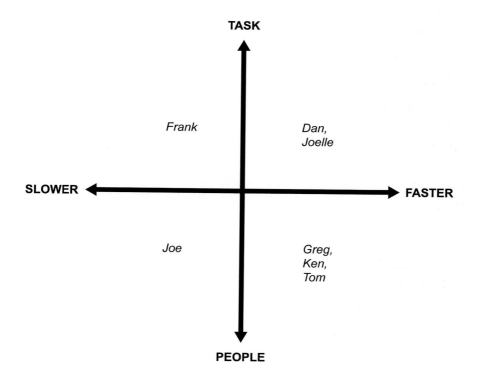

"Now the question I have for you is this: what if your natural style of selling does not match your customer's natural style for buying? What do you think that would do to the customer?"

Jack could see that some members of the team were not sure what he was driving at, so he decided to try another tack.

"I want each of you to take a few minutes and write down the way you prefer to interact with a salesperson when buying goods and/or services."

Jack waited as they considered this new question and wrote down their responses. As he expected, everyone was waiting for Frank and Joe to finish, some more impatiently than others.

Jack brought the group back together and asked Dan and Joelle what they had come up with. They both seemed to want things to be fast and to the point, not wasting their time.

Next, Jack asked Greg, Ken, and Tom their preference. They wanted a salesperson to be friendly, enthusiastic, and would like the salesperson to not be too serious.

Joe saw things differently. He wanted a salesperson that was warm and friendly. One that took the time to really understand what he was looking for. Sincere.

Frank wanted a salesperson that presented solutions in a detailed manner once they had spent the time ensuring that they understood what his needs were.

Jack summarized their responses on the graph they had created.

"So this is how you would like to have a salesperson work with you," said Jack as he motioned to the board. "What do you think would happen if that same salesperson did the exact opposite of what you desired? Would you feel frustrated?" he asked.

"For sure," replied Joe.

"You see, when we sell to others in our natural style, we connect with some people and frustrate others."

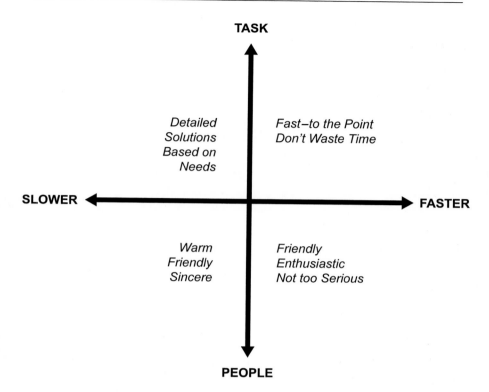

Jack turned to the team. "What do you think happens to you when someone tries to sell to you in the opposite style of what you desire? Let's take an example. Joe, you prefer to be sold to in a warm, friendly, sincere manner. Now, take a look across the grid diagonally, and tell me how it would make you feel if you were sold to by a person who was really fast, who seemed to be in a hurry?"

Joe looked at the board for a moment and then over to Jack. "I would feel like they were rushing me, and I would probably politely excuse myself and go elsewhere."

"You see, when we sell in our natural style, we connect with some customers, some customers may be mildly frustrated, and some will be very frustrated. What we need to understand as a team is how to recognize when our natural style of interacting is not what the customer would prefer, and adapt our style based on that knowledge.

In order to make this a little easier to discuss and apply, we have actually worked up some colors to describe the way each of the four styles react when they are frustrated. Here is what we have decided to use: anger – red, optimism – yellow, withdrawal – green, and fear – blue."

Jack spent some time explaining how the executive team had come up with the four colors, and why they had chosen each one. He then unveiled the graphic that he had designed based on the concept of the four faces of frustration.

The Four Faces of Frustration

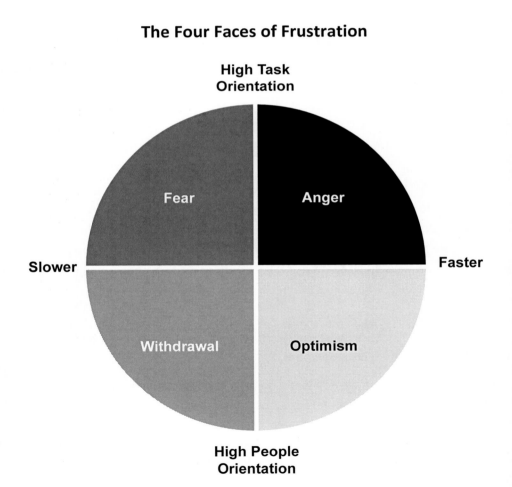

He watched the team as they absorbed what they had been working with up to this point.

Joelle spoke up first. "How are we supposed to know what style the customer is when we first meet them?" she asked.

Jack nodded. "That is a challenge. However, we give people clues to our style all the time. The first thing we need to ask is whether the person's pace of speech and action is faster or slower. That is actually the easiest thing to determine when you first meet someone. In fact, that is all I really want you to focus on for today. As you go out on your sales calls, just try to figure out the pace the customer is operating at and make an effort to adjust your pace to match that."

Jack could see heads nodding around the room. Frank, however, looked concerned. "Won't this be an inexact application of the ideas we are discussing?" he asked.

Jack nodded. "Yes, it will. However, I just want you to focus on this part of the system for today. Tomorrow, we'll meet at eight to discuss how things went and how we can use the rest of the system."

As the team filed out of the room, Jack asked Carl to stick around for a moment. He asked what his plans were for the day, and Carl told him that he had planned on riding with Dan today, as he was one of the newer reps.

"That's great," said Jack. "While you are out with him today, it is important that you also try to apply the lessons on pace that we were working on."

Carl called over his shoulder, "I'll make sure of it," as he headed out the door.

Regroup

Jack chatted with the sales team as he watched the clock. He had been pleased that Carl had arrived early enough to be in the meeting room just before eight a.m. Carl seemed to be making some progress, at least in the area of timeliness.

At eight a.m., all the sales team was present with the exception of Tom, and Jack decided that he would go ahead and get started. He began by asking each of the sales team how things had gone yesterday, specifically with their assignment of trying to determine the pace of the customers they were calling on and trying to match that pace.

Dan spoke up first.

"Well, I for one was not totally convinced that the idea of working on this was any good. However, when I called on my morning appointment I found myself noticing that the client was really moving and talking a lot slower than is my natural pace. My normal reaction would have been to try to get her to speed up, but after our meeting yesterday, I decided to keep my pace slower. It was a little painful for me."

A few of the other members of the sales team chuckled softly at this, as Dan had a bit of a reputation as a bulldozer. He always had some of the highest numbers on the team; however, he was not particularly tolerant of anyone that he felt was getting in his way—even if that was a client. Dan seemed to not have noticed the impact his comments had on the rest of the team.

He continued, "I think that she appreciated the fact that I let her set the pace of the meeting. In any case, she committed to a ninety-day trial of the software, and I'm not sure that I normally have that much success selling to her type."

Tom was just arriving as Dan finished speaking. Jack addressed Tom as he came in the room and let him know what they were discussing. Tom apologized for his tardiness and then asked if it would be okay if he shared his experience from yesterday. Jack nodded as Tom settled into his seat.

"Well, let me just say that while I always knew I was a talker, I thought that was the way I was supposed to sell. It really never occurred to me that it might turn some people off. On my second appointment yesterday, I was doing a follow-up on the client that I had been totally unable to connect with on the first call. I actually had wondered if it was really worth my time to go back and see him a second time. In any case, I kept the appointment, and I went in and noticed right out of the gate how quiet the guy was. I mean, he seemed to be testing me. He asked questions and didn't give me a whole lot of information. So, I slowed down and considered his questions very carefully. I gave him a whole lot more information than I would normally think I needed to provide. I always figured that I was wasting my time with all that detail. But you know, a funny thing happened when I slowed down and answered his questions with a slower pace. He started asking more questions. In fact, he seemed way more engaged and interested than he had at our first meeting."

Tom's enthusiasm suddenly vanished as he added: "And then I blew it."

"What do you mean?" asked Jack.

"Well, things were going so well, I just knew it was time to ask for the order. So I did, and he totally changed on me. He stopped interacting with me. Started telling me there was a lot more research that he needed to do, and he'd get back with me when he had time to look further into the matter—whatever that means."

Carl was the first to ask, "Why do you think that happened?"

Tom shook his head. "I don't know. It was going so well." He turned to the group and asked, "What do you think happened?"

Jack held up his hand and asked if they could hold that question until they had heard from the rest of the team. Tom nodded his head in agreement, and Jack turned his attention to Frank.

"How about you Frank? Did you have a chance to apply the system yesterday?"

Frank looked sheepish. "No, there didn't seem to be a good opportunity during the calls yesterday."

Jack nodded. "Okay. Let's circle back on that later and see what you have coming up today. How about you, Joe?"

"Well, if you recall, I was what you called a green. I like things to go a little slower and to build relationships with people along the way. One of my calls yesterday was with Stephen. I have known him for some time, and there is no question that he likes things to move fast. I have never been able to get him to slow down long enough to get him to consider the benefits of our solutions. So yesterday, I tried a different tack. I went in and asked him questions. I let him talk as fast as he wanted, and I didn't interrupt. In fact, there were times I really wanted to ask questions to clarify what he was saying, but I didn't. We met for about twenty minutes, and although I still don't think he understands everything we can offer him, he agreed to move forward with an analysis of his current systems and how we might improve their operating efficiency. I still don't understand how he made the decision on so little detail, but there it is."

Joe looked up at the team. It was clear that the decision-making process Stephen had used made no sense to him.

Jack continued to debrief the previous day with the rest of the sales team. Most of them had made the effort to vary the pace with which they interacted with their prospective clients. However, not all of them had. It was Jack's hope that after hearing how their peers had been successful, they would be encouraged to make the effort as well.

Jack knew it was time to move onto the next phase of the training.

"Alright, now that we have seen that the pace with which we interact with our customers has a significant impact on the likelihood of their wanting to engage with us, I want to consider the other part of the system that I shared with you yesterday."

Jack walked up to the whiteboard and pointed to the model that he had drawn there the day before.

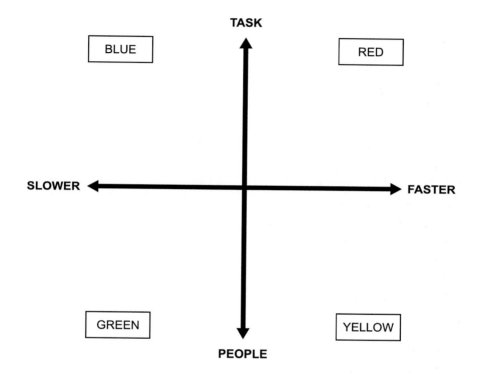

"The other part of the system was the Task–People line, and sometimes that is a little harder to determine, but not always."

Jack turned to Dan. "When you were telling us about the sales call that ended well, the one where you slowed down quite a bit, would you say that potential customer is more people- or task-focused?"

Dan considered the question briefly then responded, "I'm not sure. She seemed to be interested in getting things done, but I think she respected the fact that I spent some time getting to know her before we talked business. Is that normal?" he asked Jack.

"I think so," responded Jack. "I think very few people would just be purely one particular style. We are probably a mix of at least a couple of the different styles. I think the key thing here was the pace that you interacted with her allowed you to maintain rapport and gain a commitment for the ninety-day trial."

Dan thought about that for a moment. "So maybe she was a green-blue?" he asked.

Jack nodded. "That seems likely. However, the key here isn't to necessarily identify the color of the person, it is to make sure that we avoid behaviors that are definitely not part of the way the customer buys."

Dan thought about that for a moment. "You know. If I did this with clients that have a slower pace, I think I would have to make fewer promises to vary our basic software configuration. I think I sometimes have to promise more because I am trying to move the customer faster than they are comfortable with. Half the time we find out that the things they thought they needed could have been accomplished within our basic framework."

Jack thought about that. He had suspected as much; however, to have one of the sales team voice the matter in front of his peers was more than he could have hoped for. Jack decided that he would be understated in his response. "That's an interesting thought, Dan. I wonder if that could be true in other cases as well?"

Jack turned to Tom. "Let's think about the question that you asked earlier. Things were going well on your appointment, up to a point. What do you think happened when you asked for the order?"

Tom grimaced. "I don't know. I wish I did. I know I am people-focused. Do you think I tried to use the rapport I had established to close the sale too soon?"

Jack looked up at the board. "Perhaps so. Do you think he was more people-focused or task-focused?"

Tom answered, "Definitely more task focused. Very little chitchat from him."

Jack nodded. "So he was a task-focused, slower mover. That would make him a blue. Based on what we determined yesterday, a blue is looking for a detailed solution based on needs."

Jack turned to Frank. "Frank, you had a somewhat blue orientation, right?"

Frank nodded.

Jack continued, "If you had been in that customer's shoes, what do you think happened?"

Frank looked a little uncomfortable to have been drawn into the conversation. He cleared his throat as he considered his response.

"Well, I can't say for sure, of course. I think it is possible that you were connecting with him when you were answering questions in detail. Maybe when you started rushing things and asked for the order, he felt that you were not going to help him determine the right way to proceed and he would have to figure things out himself."

"That sounds like what happened," remarked Tom. "But I was trying to help him. I know that the solution I was proposing would have improved their capabilities."

"Perhaps," replied Frank. "But maybe he didn't feel as certain."

Jack looked around at the assembled team.

"How about you, Joe? Where do you think your customer falls on the Task–People line?"

"I have been thinking about that since yesterday. I think that he was more interested in getting things done than in building a relationship with me, so I would say more task–oriented," answered Joe.

"I think that is probably right," said Jack.

Jack walked over to the whiteboard and looked at the model one more time.

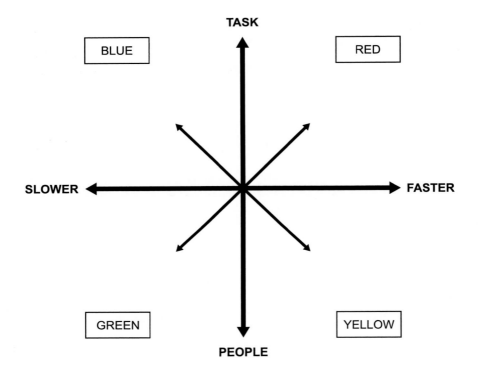

"It occurs to me that maybe the hardest people for us to understand are the people that are the exact opposite of us. Joe, since you are a green, for you that would be the reds. That's because we do not see things the same as them. Not in pace orientation or in Task–People either. It's almost like they are in our shadow, and we can't see or understand them clearly."

The meeting continued with Jack asking the different team members to share their experiences and how they thought they could use the model to help them gain more and higher quality customer commitments.

By the end of the meeting, Jack felt that they had made significant progress. He asked the team to start considering both the Task–People and pace orientation of their prospects in their sales calls from now on, and to work on keeping their prospects within the normal framework of their product offerings, rather than make special allowances that would tie the IT team in knots. He could see that they were not convinced that they could maintain their current sales numbers under those conditions.

Jack knew it was a big gamble he was taking. He just hoped that he could get the sales numbers to stabilize before he attracted too much attention from the board.

CHAPTER SEVEN

Backlash

Four weeks had passed since the first meeting where Jack had introduced the four faces model to the sales team. Jack had seen a distinct change in the results that the team was producing. Appointments seemed to be producing better quality commitments from customers, and sales had not dropped as sharply as he had feared. While the decline was not drastic, for a company that was already losing money, a decline in sales was sure to attract attention from a number of areas.

Jack had been half expecting that he might get some calls from board members; however, the nature of the calls still surprised him.

It was ten p.m. and Jack was deep in conversation with his wife. Her initial excitement at the prospect of his taking over at AmeriSys had changed to a mild resentment at the amount of time he needed to spend on the business. He had been missing meals and the kids' events on a regular basis, and he could make no promises about how soon things would improve.

The timing of a call from Jerry was unexpected, not to mention doing nothing to enhance his wife's mood. Jack apologized to Jenny as he walked to the den to try and focus on the call.

Jerry had been on the board since the company's inception. Jack had heard through the grapevine that he had not been in favor of Jack becoming CEO. He had apparently felt that Sally was a better fit to fix the problems at AmeriSys. Jack had been around the board long enough to know that Jerry was not just a single vote. He had a lot of sway with the other board members, so a call from him needed to be handled carefully.

Never one to beat about the bush, Jerry got right to the matter at hand.

"Jack, I assume you have seen the sales numbers for last month?"

Jack took a deep breath and responded that he had.

Not missing a beat, Jerry continued. "Jack, I don't think I have to remind you that cash is king in business. It's hard to fix a profitability issue when your revenues are drying up. On top of that, I understand that you have not been receptive to some key ideas from Sally about things that appear to need to be fixed right away."

Jerry paused and then continued, "Jack, what am I supposed to tell the board when we meet later this week?"

Jack took a deep breath. It wasn't that Jerry wanted him to fail, it was just that their methods were never going to align. Jack could only hope that he would be able to turn around the results at AmeriSys before Jerry was able to turn enough of the board to his point of view.

Jack looked at nothing in particular and tried to choose his words carefully. "Jerry, I realize that the sales numbers are down. As I know you are aware, the challenges at AmeriSys are numerous and are going to take some time to fix. I expect that you will start to see positive results in the near future, which I know is what the board is looking for. In the meantime, I am using my best judgment as to which challenges must be addressed first. I really appreciate the support of the board, and I look forward to having better results to report as we move forward."

Jerry was obviously not convinced. However, he was not going to press Jack further at this point. Clearly he had expected Jack to be more receptive to his advice.

"Jack, I recommend you start listening to the members of your staff that have a greater sense of urgency." The thinly veiled threat was not lost on Jack as he thanked Jerry for his call.

He hung up the phone and sat wondering, not for the first time, what he had gotten himself into. Then he went looking for Jenny. She was already in bed and appeared to be asleep. *Great,* thought Jack, *we finally get a few moments to talk, and even that time gets robbed from me by the business.* Of course, he knew that was exactly what was bothering Jenny as well.

The Customer Service Team

Jack sat at his desk the next morning and pondered the call from Jerry. He felt strongly that he was on the right path with the sales group. Sales were down, but the team was making far fewer promises for customization, so the profitability of the work they were closing would inevitably be higher.

He had decided not to try and convince Jerry of the logic of the plan that he had put in place with the team. He had no doubt that Jerry had been informed of Sally's take on the plan, and there was little that Jack could do to change Jerry's mind, short of delivering the results that he was looking for.

With the sales group creating a little less customized work for the IT group, and fewer angry customers for the customer service group, it was time to turn his attention to phase two of his plan: the customer service team.

He had scheduled the first team meeting with customer service for eight thirty. It was his intention to spend a half hour with them before the call volume really started to ramp up at nine.

The room was already quite full when Jack arrived, which he took as a good sign. He knew that many of the sales team would have shared what they had been doing with them, and so the introduction of the four faces model should be a little easier this second time through. In addition, he was starting to gain a lot of confidence in the approach.

John spent a few minutes letting the team know what they were going to work on, as well as the positive effect that he felt these ideas had on the sales team. Jack could see that some members of the customer service team were nodding in agreement, while a number of others seemed skeptical.

When John was finished with his introduction, Jack took some time to thank him and let the team know how much he appreciated how hard they worked on the phones every day.

Jack had given a lot of thought as to how to deal with the customer service team. Not only did they handle challenges with the deployment of the software, they also handled the ongoing support of the product as well. As such, the team was significantly larger than the sales team. Jack was not entirely certain that they were staffed correctly. It seemed to him that they had a larger number of reps for the size of the company and the support issues than was reasonable to expect. However, staffing was an issue that would need to be addressed at a later time. If he could get things running smoother in sales, there would be fewer crises to handle in customer service, and perhaps parts of the team could be redeployed to add value elsewhere.

After introducing the four faces model, Jack led the team through the exercise that assisted each team member in assessing what their natural style would be. When the grid was completed, Jack stood back so that the entire team could see what they had come up with:

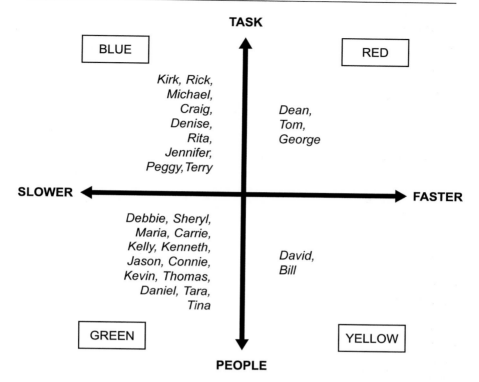

As Jack had expected, there was heavy slant toward the green-blue side of the grid. He suspected this had to do with the need for the reps to handle a lot of repetitive, detail-oriented work that was better suited to the behaviors represented by those colors.

The challenge would be in getting the reps to understand the unique challenges associated in dealing with their red and yellow customers, not to mention the fact that he had at least five reps that would be a mismatch for the customers that had a green-blue orientation.

Jack led the customer service team through a similar exercise to the one that he had utilized with the sales team. Jack addressed the team, "Let's talk about what great customer service means to each of the four colors represented in the room here. Let's start with the red group. What does great customer service look like to you when you call in to a company whose product you have purchased?"

Dean was the first to speak up. "What I want is someone who is knowledgeable and does not waste my time. I want to get off the phone ASAP."

Jack could see the rest of the red group nodding in agreement, while there were a few of the members of the green group that had wrinkled their brows as they listened to the reds. While he had begun to expect this reaction from different groups, he still found it remarkable that such a simple concept could produce such predictable results.

Jack then turned to the yellow group. "How about you? What does great customer service look like to you?"

David and Bill looked at each other and smiled back at Jack. David was the first to speak up.

"I want someone who is going to help me out and not waste my time as well." He glanced over at the reds and then added, "I guess a little bit of personality doesn't hurt either. I just want to have a little fun as well."

Jack turned to the green group. They were clearly the largest color represented in the room with more than fifteen in their group.

"What about the greens? What does great customer service look like to you?"

An uncomfortable silence followed Jack's question. The voice that Jack heard next did not come from the greens; it came from the yellow corner.

"I think they want things to move slower," remarked Bill.

Jack smiled as he looked over at Bill. He knew a "teaching moment" when one smacked him in the face. "Bill, let me ask you a question. Why did you feel it necessary to help the greens out with my question?"

Jack could see that his question had caught Bill off guard. Not desiring to embarrass Bill, Jack added, "You were trying to help, weren't you?"

Bill nodded. "Yes. It seemed like they were having difficulty speaking up."

Jack nodded. "One of the things that the reds and yellows need to recognize is that the greens and blues do take a little longer to process and answer questions sometimes. However, we need to strongly resist the urge to answer for them. Although we might not intend it, it may feel disrespectful to them at times."

Jack could see a number of the greens and blues nodding in agreement.

"Okay, so let's go back to the greens. What does great customer service look like to you?"

This time the greens seemed to be ready to answer his question. Harry piped up, "I like someone to listen to my answers and make sure they understand what is happening before they start trying to solve my problem."

Most of the greens and some of the blues were nodding.

"I see," said Jack. "And what about the blues? What does great customer service look like to you?"

After what Jack knew was an uncomfortable silence to the reds and yellows, Kirk spoke up.

"I don't know about everyone else, but I like to speak to someone who is knowledgeable and doesn't waste my time with a lot of questions that are not relevant to the problem I am trying to solve."

Jack looked back at the group. "As we just saw, we all define great customer service slightly differently. The natural implication of this is that we also tend to try to serve clients the way we would want to be treated. Right?"

Jack could see most of the heads in the room nodding in agreement.

"Let's see if we can summarize what we have discussed so far."

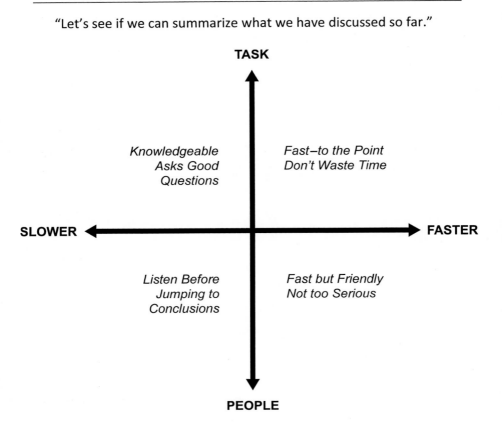

TASK

Knowledgeable
Asks Good
Questions

Fast—to the Point
Don't Waste Time

SLOWER ← → **FASTER**

Listen Before
Jumping to
Conclusions

Fast but Friendly
Not too Serious

PEOPLE

Jack stood back and looked at the grid they had created and addressed the team. "What do you think happens when someone tries to serve us in exactly the opposite way we would define great customer service? In other words, if you look across the grid diagonally, you will see that the way people define customer service seems to be almost the opposite of one another. You would likely feel frustrated, wouldn't you?"

"I know I do when I feel people are moving too slow," volunteered George. "Sometimes I feel like I could do their job better than they can!"

Jack laughed to relieve the tension of the moment and asked George, "Do you think it is possible that when that happens, you are just dealing with a person who is trying to serve you really well and is trying to make sure they understand the situation fully before they advise you on a solution?"

"Perhaps," replied George, "but it sure is frustrating."

"And therein lies the lesson for us all," replied Jack. "What we need to understand as a team is how to recognize when our natural style of interacting is not what the customer would prefer, and adapt our style based on that knowledge. In order to make this a little easier to discuss and apply, we have actually worked up some colors to describe the way each of the four styles react when they are frustrated. Here is what we have decided to use: anger – red, optimism – yellow, withdrawal – green, and fear – blue."

Jack spent some time explaining how the executive team had come up with the four colors, and why they had chosen each one. He then unveiled the graphic that he had designed based on the concept of the four faces of frustration.

"The challenge for us in customer service is that we only talk to our customers we don't often meet them. So we need to learn how to assess their behavioral style based on what we hear on the phone. However, we give people clues to our style all the time. The first thing we need to ask is whether the person's pace of speech and action is faster or slower. That is actually the easiest thing to determine when you first meet someone. In fact, that is all I really want you to focus on while you are on the phones today. Just try to figure out the pace the customer is operating at and make an effort to adjust your pace to match that."

Jack could see heads nodding around the room. "Tomorrow, we will meet at eight to discuss how things went and how we can use the rest of the system."

As the team filed out of the room, Jack asked John to stick around for a moment. He asked John how he felt things had gone in the meeting. John hesitated for a moment and shifted his weight from one foot to the other.

"I think it went great. In fact, I wanted to let you know that we are all feeling a lot less pressure these days based on the changes that have occurred in the sales group. I really feel that the success we are experiencing over there made this meeting much easier. In fact, many of my people have been asking for some time when they were going to get a chance to learn the four faces system. Jack, I know that we have a lot of challenges to address here at AmeriSys. But for the first time in a while, I'm really starting to feel like it's all going to work out."

Jack smiled at John. "I am too. Please let me know if you experience any challenges before tomorrow morning."

Round Two

Jack knew that the eight o'clock start time would cause some challenges for some members of the customer service team, so he began the meeting by expressing his sincere appreciation to all of them for coming in a little earlier than normal. He would have preferred not to have to ask people to come in earlier; however, their workday started when the phones went live at nine, and they could not afford to have customers getting a voice mail message that they would be called back at such a critical time.

Jack began by asking the team how things had gone on the phones yesterday. Had they been able to pick up on their customers' natural pace, and had they been able to then make changes and match that pace?

Not surprisingly, it was Bill, a yellow, who spoke up first.

"I was actually shocked at how easy it was to pick up on this sometimes, and at other times it was much harder."

"Tell us more, Bill," responded Jack.

"Well. I took a number of calls that would normally be painful for me. The customer was really detailed and seemed to be missing the 'big picture.' However, I remembered what we talked about yesterday and slowed down and tried to match their pace. I have to tell you that the calls seemed to go better, but it drove me nuts!" Bill shook his head and looked back at Jack as if to say "what now?"

Jack nodded. "Why was it sometimes hard to tell what the customer's desired pace was?" he asked.

Bill shook his head. "I don't know. Some people seemed to alter their pace based on what we were talking about. Is that normal?"

"I think it is," responded Jack. "You see, most of us have at least two colors that influence the way we like to interact with people. I know we have been talking about being just one color, but that was more for the simplicity of understanding the system than anything else."

Terry (a blue) asked, "Can you have more than two colors present in your behavioral style?"

"Oh sure," replied Jack. "All four colors are represented within each of us to one degree or another. It's just that one or two tend to be more prevalent—especially when we are under a lot of stress."

Jack hesitated for a moment and then said to Bill, "You mentioned earlier that when you were able to adjust your pace to meet the needs of the client that the call went better—but that it drove you nuts."

"That's right," replied Bill.

Jack returned his attention to the group. "One of the things that we need to really work on as a team is acting the way that customers need us to, even when it's hard for us."

He returned his attention to Bill. "So thank you for doing the right thing even when it is hard. You see, the natural way for Bill to handle that client, and much less stressful for him, would have been to rush things along—perhaps even finishing a few sentences for the customer. However, that would not have been delivering great customer service. I know that this is hard. It does get easier over time.

93

But there is some really hard work to do before this starts feeling more natural. Did any of you experience needing to speed up as you handled customer calls?"

Jack knew that based on the makeup of the customer service group, this would be the biggest challenge they would need to address. There was a brief but painful silence, and Jack was glad to see that the reds and yellows allowed the silence to continue, even when it appeared to become painful for a few of them.

When it became apparent that Jack did not intend to continue until someone shared, Craig cleared his throat and spoke up.

"I certainly saw the difference in pace," he began.

"Tell us more," encouraged Jack.

"Well, it seems that a lot of the calls we get are from customers who are frustrated. I think when they are frustrated, their 'colors' really show."

This elicited a laugh from the whole group. Obviously encouraged, Craig continued. "I noticed on one call in particular that the customer was really rushing things. They seemed to be really upset, so I'm thinking they were maybe a red. In any case, my natural reaction would have been to try and get the customer to slow down so I could get the details I needed to solve the problem. But, based on what you told us yesterday, I figured that would just make him angrier."

"So what did you do?" asked Jack.

Craig looked sheepish. "I stopped trying to enter all the data in the system and just talked to him for a few minutes. The more I listened and responded to his questions quickly, the more he seemed to settle down. Then eventually I was able to get the data into the system and ask the questions that helped me solve his problem. The crazy thing is that I could have helped him faster if he would have listened to me. But he didn't want to."

Craig shook his head in bewilderment.

Jack nodded. "Craig's experience is a great example of making sure that you are aligned with the customer before you ask them to change their pace. He could get the customer to slow down once the customer felt they were being heard—but until you match the customer's pace, you are just going to frustrate them further—even if you are really trying to help them."

"So we don't have to change our pace for the whole call?" asked Jennifer.

"I don't think so," responded Jack. "You may still move faster than is comfortable for you, but it doesn't have to be at light speed once you have aligned with the customer and they know that they have been heard."

Jack could sense a feeling of relief from many of the team.

"We discussed yesterday that pace orientation is the easiest thing to pick up on, especially on the phone. The other part of the four faces model was the Task–People orientation. That can be a harder thing to pick up on, especially on the phone. Does anyone have an example of a call yesterday where you think you could figure their Task–People orientation out?"

"Oh yeah," replied Rick. Rick was a blue, and Jack had yet to hear from him in the training sessions. "I took a call just before lunch yesterday, and I immediately got a sense that this guy was a fast talker. But the truth was, even though he was talking fast, he seemed to take a long time to say anything. And he kept shooting off on tangents that were completely unrelated to what we were discussing."

"Where do you think he was on the Task–People line?" asked Jack.

"Well, I don't think a red would have talked so much, especially about unrelated stuff—so I think he was more people-oriented. That would make him a yellow, right?" asked Rick.

Jack and most of the group could not help looking over at the yellows, who were sitting speechless at the way they had just been described. Knowing that humor is often the best way to diffuse times like these, Jack smiled and genuinely offered, "I bet you didn't know that you could come across that way—did you?"

Everyone had a good laugh.

Jack took some time to explain the concept of the "shadow side" that they had formulated with the sales team.

He explained that the "shadow side" is the color that is opposite to you. He sketched out the pairings on the board:

RED – GREEN

YELLOW – BLUE

Jack continued, "As you deal with your customers on the phone, your biggest challenges will be with those individuals from your shadow side. In fact, if you find yourself or the customer becoming frustrated by the way the call is going, there is a good likelihood that person is from your shadow side. These are the customers that will be the hardest to work with, but if we can learn how to shift our focus and treat them in a way that they feel is 'great customer service,' then we will experience far less stress, and our customers will feel more valued."

The nine a.m. deadline loomed large on the group, so Jack took a few minutes to let them know how much he appreciated their time and attention. He asked them to continue to apply the four faces model in their interactions with their customers.

After the meeting broke up, Jack returned to his office and made a few notes about how he would need to follow up with the customer service group. He felt encouraged by the progress that was being made in the customer-facing parts of the organization.

That left two areas that needed his time and attention. IT and administration. Jack felt a knot in his stomach as he considered the challenge of working with Sally. She was, quite possibly, the most challenging personality that he had ever met. On top of that, she had clear support from within the board and seemed to be more than willing to use her pipeline to certain board members to challenge his authority.

What he really needed was a plan.

CHAPTER EIGHT

When It Rains It Pours

Jack drove home from work that day with the nagging feeling that he had forgotten something. He ran through his day in his mind. The customer service meeting had gone quite well. John seemed to be getting significant traction with the team implementing the four faces system, and the initial signs were that customer satisfaction with the support team was on the upswing. The sales team continued to make progress with their sales goals. They were still off target, but less so than the week before, and the quality of work was increasing as they were making fewer commitments for custom work. He had yet to decide how to work through the myriad challenges with IT and administration. He shook his head; that wasn't it, though.

There was something else. Right at the edge of his mind. He couldn't shake the feeling that something important was being missed.

It was almost dark as he turned into his driveway. He stared at the house and wondered why there were no lights on. Then suddenly it hit him. The charity fundraiser for the school was tonight. Jenny had reminded him just this morning that he would need to meet her no later than six p.m. at the school so that he could assist with the kids and help her with the last-minute set up of the gym.

How could he have been so stupid?

He looked at his watch and grimaced as he saw it was already seven p.m. The event would already be starting. Although Jenny always tried to be understanding with the demands that his job put on him and the family, this was one time when she had specifically asked for him to make her a priority.

And he had blown it.

He backed the car out of the driveway and dialed Jenny on his cell as he sped down the street. No answer. Well, what did he expect? She would be hip-deep in things by now.

Jenny would be furious. No, she would be hurt. That was actually harder for Jack than if she was just mad at him. He had let her down.

Somehow he had to find a way to balance the demands of his new job and his commitment to the most important people in his life.

Jenny was even busier than he had expected, and Jack never had a moment to speak with her until they were cleaning up later that night. The mood was tense as they stacked chairs together. Jack decided this was as good a time as any to apologize.

"I'm so sorry, Jenny. Forgetting the event was tonight was thoughtless of me. I know I have to do a better job of making sure you and the kids are a priority in my schedule."

Jenny had stopped stacking chairs and was looking at him. "Yes, you do. Look, I understand what you are going through at work. But the kids don't. All they see is an empty chair at dinner and all their events." She started stacking chairs again. "Don't get me wrong. I'm not saying I don't care. Just please tell me that this is not the new normal for us."

Jack went over to her and took her hands in his. "No, it's not. I can't promise you that this will all be over tomorrow or next week. But I can promise you this: If we can't get the company to where it needs to be in the next three to four months, where you and I can see some improvement, then we need to have a long chat about whether this was a big mistake."

Jenny looked at him and asked, "Do you think it will come to that?"

Jack shook his head. "No," he answered, "I don't. But at the same time, I am under a lot of pressure from the board to make changes that I believe with all my heart are the wrong way to go. I think the next few months will either show the kind of positive progress that we all need to see, or...well...it won't."

Jenny looked at him. "Don't doubt yourself now, Jack. I can handle the kids for a few more months. You make sure the doubters end up eating crow. You understand?"

Jack nodded. "Thanks, honey."

He gave her a big hug. Jenny smiled and said, "Let's get this mess cleaned up, okay?"

Fireworks

Jack made a point of getting the kids up for school the next morning and joking around with them as they went through the morning routine. He was still smiling as he pulled into the parking lot at AmeriSys, but the smile vanished from his face as he saw a large Mercedes parked out front.

Great, thought Jack. I come in a little later one day, and that is the day a key board member chooses to show up.

Never one to shy away from controversy, Jerry had made a point of parking in the "employee of the month" parking spot. Jack could see that Andy was parked off to the right. Andy had won the honor for exceeding his sales quota the previous month and really putting into play many of the lessons from the four faces model.

Jack parked in his usual spot and headed into the building, wondering where he would find Jerry and what other fires he would have set smoldering this early in the morning.

He needn't have bothered wondering. The answer was evident as soon as he walked in the door. Jack found Jerry engaged in a deep conversation with Sam. Sam was being his usual calm and thoughtful self, while Jerry was looking a little agitated.

Jack smiled at both of them as he approached. Jerry stepped back from his dialogue with Sam and for a moment looked for all the world like he had been caught in the midst of something he shouldn't have been doing.

Jack shook both of their hands and said good morning. Jerry greeted him stiffly and asked if he could have a few minutes of his time. Jack was still wondering what they had been discussing, agreed, and proceeded up to his office while making small talk with Jerry. He could see Fran's eyebrows rise almost imperceptibly as he and Jerry walked toward his office.

"Good morning, Fran," remarked Jack with what he hoped was his best "not to worry" smile.

The truth was, Jack was perhaps a little worried by Jerry's sudden appearance. He had only ever seen one board member visit outside of actual board meetings, and that had been the man who had walked him into the building, the chairman of the board, Gary.

Jack dropped his briefcase next to his desk and asked Jerry if he would like anything to drink. Jerry declined, so Jack closed the office door and went to sit with Jerry at the newly installed "old" conference table. If Jerry noticed the change, he did not make any comment.

"I'm sure you're wondering why I came in today, so I'll get right to the point," Jerry began.

Jack leaned back and tried to remember all the lessons he had learned on how to deal with Jerry's type. Clearly he was a red, but Jack suspected he had a lot of blue (detail orientation) in his style as well. He would need to stay on task and not take things personally as Jerry spoke.

Jerry continued, "I have heard some disturbing things out of the sales group recently. When we spoke the other night, I let you know of my concerns with the sales numbers. What I did not know is that the decrease was due to actually turning down work with customers that need a little extra attention. Jack, I want to give you every opportunity to succeed. However, as you were told at the outset, we have a very short time frame to turn this company around. And if the company becomes even less profitable than it was, that will impact how we are valued in any possible buyout scenario. Why would you have a policy of turning down work when we clearly need the business?"

Jerry had barely taken a breath.

Jack leaned forward and nodded his head. "It's true that we have become more selective in our sales process. However, I would not say that we are turning away that much work at all. More often than not, in working with the customer, we can make a sale without promising a tremendous amount of customization work that ties our IT team in knots, or worse yet, that we cannot deliver."

Jack sat back in his chair and studied Jerry. Where was he getting his information from? It had to be Sally. He would have to address her inability to work as a team sooner or later. And based on this conversation, it was likely to be sooner rather than later.

Jack decided to press Jerry a little for information. "Tell me, Jerry, where did the impression that we are turning work down come from?"

Jerry cocked his head to the side as if he could not understand the question. "The fact that you are asking me this question tells me that the person who spoke to me has not come to you with their concern. So rather than tell you who it was, I want you to consider the three possibilities of why that may be: One, they don't trust you and don't think you will give them a fair hearing. Two, they are actively trying to undermine you as CEO. Or three, both of the above."

Jerry stood up and looked at Jack.

"Look, Jack. While it is true that you were not my first choice for CEO here, I also do not want to see you fail. I know you think you are on the right track, and for all of our sakes, I hope you are correct. However, if you do not have the trust of your senior team, then I would say the chances of success are diminished."

Jack stood. "I need to know who it was," he said.

Jerry shook his head. "I don't know whether it is a trust issue or not. You have to figure that out. And I'm not going to make it worse by violating a trust placed in me just in case it is a trust issue." Jerry placed his hand on Jack's shoulder. "Remember, trust is not easily earned. It may not be the issue here, but that is what you are going to have to figure out."

After Jerry left, Jack pondered the feedback he had received. Apparently he had a bigger problem than he had initially perceived. There was a soft knock at the door, and Jack mumbled, "Come in."

Sam popped his head around the half-open door. "Sorry, boss," he said. "I never got to your office before you came in, as I got caught in the lobby with Jerry."

Jack was not in the least surprised to hear Sam, the janitor, addressing a member of the board on a first-name basis. Jack smiled and waved Sam in.

"By the way, Sam. If it's not violating a confidence, what were you and Jerry talking about when I arrived?"

Sam smiled that funny half smile he had when he was up to something. "Oh, that," he began. "Jerry likes to push people around sometimes. I don't think he means anything by it; he just gets focused on his goal and can sometimes run people over in the process."

Jack nodded. "A red, wouldn't you say?"

"Flaming red," replied Sam with a chuckle.

"So what was he looking all worked up about?" asked Jack.

Sam took a breath. "Years ago I was Jerry's Sunday school teacher at church."

"Really?" asked Jack. "I'll bet that was an interesting class."

"Yes, it was," replied Sam. "Jerry was a hard charger even back then. I loved to talk to them about 'life lessons.' I felt it necessary to remind him of one of them this morning. And he didn't like it any more today than when he was a youngster."

"What was it?" asked Jack.

"That you should always be loyal to the absent. In other words, always make sure that you do not say anything about someone that you would not say directly to them. Most people will say lots about you when you are not around, but clam up when it's time to talk directly."

"Why did that bother Jerry?"

Sam hesitated, and then decided he would not violate his own rules by responding. "Because he was intent on figuring out what is happening around here, and he was asking me to betray the confidence of people that let me into their offices with the expectation that I will not repeat what I overhear. He told me 'they would never know.' That's when I reminded him of the life lesson."

Sam shook his head. "He didn't like it. Said he was only trying to help. And I believe he really was."

Jack asked, "Did you just violate you own rule by telling me this?"

"Nope," replied Sam. "I am tremendously loyal to Jerry. He was and still is one of my favorite students I ever taught. In fact, I will likely tell him of this exact conversation the next time I see him."

"You really are a rare bird. You know that, don't you?" asked Jack.

Sam chuckled. "I'll take that as a compliment."

"Can I ask for some advice?" asked Jack.

"Sure, as long as I can clean as we talk." Sam busied himself with the trash as Jack considered how to proceed.

He decided to tell Sam of the entire conversation he had with Jerry and of Jerry's thoughts on why the problem had surfaced. He also let him know that Jerry would not tell him who his source was.

"Personally, I think it's Sally. She has been gunning for me ever since I arrived. What do you think I should do?" asked Jack.

"Well, let's consider how each of the 'four faces' build trust and how they typically deal with disagreement. The reds are easy to read. You build trust with them by being good at what you do and delivering on time. Reds deal with disagreement directly. They are a pain in the butt, but you always know where you stand with them."

Jack frowned. "Based on that analysis, it wouldn't be Sally, would it?"

Sam shook his head. "Let's not forget that behavior is only one element of who you are. You can't make sweeping statements from behavior alone. People are motivated by many things."

"Okay," said Jack. "The yellows."

"Yes," said Sam, "they are more difficult to read. They give trust freely and expect that others should do the same. However, they deal with disagreement less directly. They often try to persuade themselves, and others, that there is actually agreement. They can find it hard to address disagreement directly."

Sam continued, "The greens are often the hardest to read. They build trust very slowly based on a long track record and personal relationship. They are incredibly loyal once trust is established. However, it is a hard climb to establish it. They dislike conflict and therefore find it hard to speak openly about disagreement unless it is something they are passionate about.

"Lastly, the blues. They build trust slowly like the greens. However, they base their decision on trust more on logic and whether they can see a case for competence over the long run. They have no difficulty discussing disagreement, especially in factual terms. They don't make it personal."

Jack went up to his trusty whiteboard and wrote his direct reports on the board.

Sally (Administration/Finance) – Red

Carl (Sales) – Yellow

John (Customer Service) – Green

Bob (IT) – Blue

He had overwhelming urge to follow his instincts. It had to be Sally. Didn't it? But reds were more direct.

Jack peered over at Sam. "You already know, don't you?"

Sam said, "Loyal to the absent," and crossed his heart.

"Is it possible that the person did not think they were stirring up trouble, and they were just talking? Perhaps concerned they were going to be judged as lacking if I failed?"

"I suppose anything is possible; why do you ask?" asked Sam.

Jack stood back and looked at the board. "I'm feeling frustrated with Sally, and I was ready to jump to conclusions it was her. But I think that it is just as likely it was Carl. Yellows can talk a lot, and sometimes may speak out of turn and not even know they have. Jerry, as a red, would likely have no difficulty getting information out of him."

Jack turned to see Sam smiling. "It really could be anyone, Jack. I think the lesson here is that just because someone is difficult to manage doesn't make them untrustworthy."

"You mean Sally," nodded Jack.

Sam tilted his head in agreement.

Jack watched as Sam wheeled his cart out the door and proceeded with his duties.

Support

Jack decided to wander down to the sales department first to see whether the numbers were continuing to improve. He found Carl deep in conversation in his office with Tricia, a top performer. Jack waited patiently and busied himself chatting with other members of the sales team.

Tricia barely glanced at him as she came out of Carl's office. Carl looked sheepish as he welcomed Jack in.

"Carl," began Jack, "is something wrong with Tricia?"

"It's her numbers. Her performance is way off ever since we started on this new policy of not making exceptions for clients. She is having a difficult time adjusting, and her numbers are off to another bad start this month. I had to tell her that things were going to have to turn around, or else we would have to do something different."

Jack pulled his hand through his hair. "Carl, this sort of thing is simple for you, isn't it? I don't mean talking to Tricia about her performance, I mean knowing how to talk to customers and build rapport so you can understand their needs. That way you can get them to understand how our standard offering is closer than they thought to their true needs."

Carl nodded. "It doesn't really seem that hard. You just have to listen to the customer's needs and ask good questions."

Jack smiled. "Carl, have you coached Tricia on how to listen more effectively? Or have you primarily provided her with feedback as to her results?"

"I guess mostly feedback," said Carl. "But surely she knows how to listen?" asked Carl, almost incredulous that Jack had suggested it.

Jack said, "I don't know. But Tricia is a red, right?"

Carl nodded.

Jack continued. "Reds are not known to be great listeners, and they tend to be fast-paced. Perhaps she just needs some coaching?"

Carl considered the advice he had received. "It just never occurred to me she might not know how. I just thought she was being obstinate. In fact, I find quite a few of my higher performing sales reps are resistant to the new way we are trying to get them to operate. It's like our lower performing reps have stepped up their performance, and the higher performing reps are now our low performers."

Jack listened carefully, knowing that Carl, a yellow, liked to talk things through as he thought about them.

Carl looked at him. "So I need to provide better coaching to them as to how they can do the things I am asking of them, don't I?"

Jack nodded. "I think at least then you will have a better idea if it is an issue with skill or motivation, don't you?"

Carl nodded. "I think so. Thanks, boss. Hey, what did you come on down for?"

Jack chose his words carefully. "Carl, are you feeling a lot of pressure to meet the sales targets we have set forth?"

Carl didn't miss a beat. "Sure! I mean, it's my head that's going to roll first, right? I mean, no offense, but I have my highest performing people unhappy right now, and my numbers aren't looking all that great. I have board members asking questions and breathing down my neck. So yes, I can feel the heat, but I can also handle the heat. You know what I mean?"

Bingo, thought Jack. *It was Carl.* Not only that, but it wasn't the huge violation of trust that he had thought it was. He considered how quickly he had jumped to the conclusion that Sally was stirring up trouble.

Snapping back to the moment, he assured Carl that he had every confidence in his ability and asked if it would be okay if he checked in occasionally to see how the coaching was going. Carl smiled broadly at the offer and told Jack he would welcome help anywhere he could find it.

Jack left the sales group feeling better than he had since he walked into the lobby that morning.

Accountability

Jack took a walk through the customer service group on his way back to his desk. He knew he needed to start focusing on the IT and the administrative areas; however, his time in sales had reminded him how important it was to keep the momentum going once you had a group headed in the right direction.

He arrived in customer service and found John sitting at a rep's desk listening to a call and providing some sound coaching on how the rep could address customer concerns more effectively. The difference between the two coaching styles—Carl's and John's—was remarkable.

However, Jack had learned from experience that providing insight on how a needed change was to happen was only part of the solution. The other half was holding people accountable to the change. Carl had been able to execute the accountability part of the equation, to the point that Tricia had felt frustration from the conversation. Jack felt that was why she had not wanted to look at him as she left Carl's office. She was a high performer, and she was not used to failing. Worse yet, he was fairly certain that she did not know *why* she was failing. What he had asked Carl to do was to step back and address the "how" of the change with Tricia.

John was a different story altogether. As a green, John would be all about supporting his people and helping them see how to achieve their goals. What was left to be seen was whether John was able to hold people accountable to the changes that were reasonable to expect. That would require John to have some difficult conversations at times.

John was finishing his conversation with his rep. "Okay, overall I think you are doing a really good job. If you could just try to ask more questions of the customer rather than telling them what to do, I think that would help a lot."

John smiled at the rep as he got up from the desk and turned to address Jack. "Hey there. Is everything okay?"

"Absolutely," replied Jack casually. "How are things going?"

"Well," began John, "I think we are making good progress."

Jack nodded. Jack's natural style would have been to launch into a discussion of what he thought John could do differently. However, he knew that as a green, John would respond better if he gave him some time to prepare and consider what Jack wanted to discuss with him.

"That's great," replied Jack. "Would it be okay if we sat down a little later today and looked at your team and how things are going on the performance goals we set last month? What time would work best for you?"

John pulled out his schedule and frowned as he looked at the afternoon. "Well," he paused, "what about 3:30?"

Jack made a note of the time and told John that he looked forward to chatting with him later that day. As he made his way back to his office he made a mental note of what he had learned so far:

Carl (a yellow) was comfortable with providing feedback on what goals were not being achieved but avoided having the more detailed coaching conversations about what needed to be done differently to achieve those goals.

John (a green) was less comfortable with holding people accountable for reasonable changes but seemed to excel at collaborative coaching and engaging his people in the types of conversations that imparted the knowledge and skill necessary to change.

What he had noticed over his career, even before he had learned about the four colors, was that leaders tended to either be more comfortable holding people accountable or tended to be more supportive in their feedback. The four faces model gave him an opportunity to provide even more targeted feedback around the types of behaviors that each leader needed to focus on using more of.

Accountability

True to his word, Jack arrived in the customer service group at three thirty that afternoon. He found John looking over some performance data at the small conference table in his office. Jack knocked on the door and John looked up, smiled at him, and waved him over to a chair at the table.

Jack spent some time asking John about his family and how things were going. He had learned from experience that although some leaders (mostly reds and blues) found this social dialogue frustrating, others (yellows and greens) often found it a necessary part of many conversations. What was necessary was to gauge your audience and see what level of social dialogue they preferred.

With the social part of their conversation winding down, John asked Jack where he would like to start.

Jack thought for a moment. "Why don't you let me know what you are seeing from a performance perspective from your team?" asked Jack.

"Okay," began John. "We have some strong results in most of our key areas." John went on to describe the positive progress that the team had made. He then hesitated, as if unsure how, or perhaps if, he should continue. From what he had heard, Jack believed that the previous CEO's style would have been the exact opposite of John's style. His reluctance to move into areas where his group needed to improve was probably based on a wariness about how Jack would react.

John continued, "The area I have the most concern in is our service levels. We are not making as much progress as I know we are capable of. The scores show that our customers still feel like they are receiving substandard service."

Jack nodded. "Why do you feel that your team is capable of better performance in that area?"

Jack remained quiet as John considered his question. "I can see the changes that are required, and I feel I have provided solid coaching to the reps about what they need to change. However, even though they seem committed, the changes in behavior just are not happening."

John shook his head, showing his frustration for the first time. "I just am not sure what is getting in the way."

He looked up at Jack.

"Do you mind if I ask you a few questions?" began Jack.

John shrugged his shoulders. "Sure. Any help would be appreciated."

Jack had thought the situation through and so knew what he needed to ask. "When you are coaching people, do they make specific commitments as to what behaviors they are going to change?"

John thought for a moment. "I think so. We talk things through, and usually I summarize the conversation at the end." John paused. "Come to think of it though, I guess I don't actually ask for a commitment from them. Do you think that's important?"

"I think it really is," responded Jack. "What I have found is that people often have problems with what we ask them to do, and when they have to verbalize the commitment themselves, they often voice concerns that may not have been discussed otherwise."

John considered what Jack had said. "I hadn't thought of that. I wonder if that is why we aren't getting the movement on some of the changes that seem so simple to me? Thanks, Jack. I'm going to try that in my next few coaching sessions and see if people start sharing their concerns."

Jack thanked John for his time and let him know that he would check in the next day to see how things were going.

Follow-Up

Jack saw John on the way into work the next day. He didn't mention the conversation from the previous day, as he had intended to give John some additional time to have a few coaching conversations. However, to his surprise, John brought the matter up.

"You know Jack, I was a little unsure of whether what we talked about yesterday would work or not. After you left, one of the reps had a challenge, and it was a great opportunity to provide some coaching. I took your advice, and at the end I asked her what she was going to do rather than telling her. To my surprise, she was hesitant to commit to doing things differently. When I asked her why, she replied that she could not see how she could follow my advice and meet her other numbers."

"So what did you do?" asked Jack.

"Well, I stepped back into coaching mode and asked her a bunch more questions, and we talked for a while until she understood how to make the change work. I have to tell you, Jack, I think that this could have a big impact on our customer service numbers. I'm looking forward to trying this with some of the other team members that seem to be struggling to see if I get similar results."

John gave Jack a hopeful look as he headed down the hall to his office.

Instead of heading to his office, Jack first took a walk down to the sales group. He found Carl sitting with Tricia, strategizing her approach on a sales call she was to make later that day. Jack waited patiently while Carl finished up, spending his time chatting with a few of the sales reps that were milling about.

Carl wrapped up his talk and came over to greet Jack. "Hey, boss. Always good to see you."

As Carl and Jack walked toward Carl's office, Jack asked him if he had a chance to apply some of the feedback from the previous day.

Carl responded immediately, "You betcha. In fact, I thought Tricia was going to hug me when I asked if there was anything I could help her with. She told me she had resigned herself to trying to figure out the new sales process on her own. I'm a little embarrassed that I didn't see that one coming. I just figured that since she was a top performer, she would know what to do. Turns out that wasn't the case."

"I know what you mean," replied Jack. "So, do you think there are other members of your team who could benefit from additional coaching from you?"

"I know there are," jumped in Carl. "In fact, I can see now that in trying to hold them accountable without supporting them in figuring out the 'how,' I was not only frustrating myself but them as well!"

Jack smiled at Carl and let him know that he was there to assist if he could.

As Jack walked to his office, his smile faded. IT and administration. That's what he needed to work on now. And that meant dealing with Sally. She had been keeping a lower profile of late, but Jack knew that would abruptly end when he started working with her and asking her to make changes in her departments, not to mention the changes that Sally needed to make in her management style.

CHAPTER NINE

Push Back

The clock seemed to move slowly past six thirty as Jack sat at his desk pondering the approach that he should take with Sally. He actually had two department heads left to address, Sally and Bob. Jack had already decided that his next project would be Sally's group; however, he had been delaying approaching her now for almost a week. He seemed to be struggling more than usual with defining the right tactic to take with her.

He had come in earlier than normal today to get his mind around how to approach Sally. He needed some time to think without all the normal workday interruptions.

He asked himself, not for the first time, why he was struggling so much with this. The simple answer was that Sally would be far less accepting of his input than John and Carl had been.

But that wasn't the whole story. He was the CEO. He was supposed to be ready for challenges of this type. What was making him reluctant to have the hard conversation that was inevitable?

Sam's quiet knock at the door startled him. "Mind if I come in for a moment, boss?" Sam asked cheerily.

Jack waved him in. "Not at all. Come on in."

"What brings you in so early?" asked Sam.

"Sally," replied Jack. "I need to decide how I am going to address her and her group."

"Oh," replied Sam knowingly.

Jack looked at Sam. "This is my hardest one yet. I can't seem to grasp the best way to handle her. I don't want to make matters worse, and I can't really afford to lose her. Why is this one so hard for me, Sam?"

Sam stooped to pick up and empty a garbage can. "Why do you think it is?" he asked with a hint of humor in his eyes.

"She's just so pig-headed!" Jack exclaimed. "She doesn't listen, and she doesn't take advice well."

Sam nodded. "I think that she can come across that way at times, especially when she is under a lot of stress."

"But a lot of the stress would go away if she would be a little less of a driver and trust her people more."

"I agree," said Sam.

"How do you get a red to slow down and see things from a different perspective?"

Sam thought about that for a moment. "I have always found that most people listen to a very specific radio station."

Jack cocked his head to the side and looked at Sam inquisitively. "What exactly does your choice of radio station have to do with managing people?" he asked.

"Well," replied Sam, "it isn't a real radio station. Not one you tune into in your car anyway. It's WIIFM. What's In It For Me radio."

Jack laughed despite the tension he was feeling. "I see," he said as the laughter died away. "How would I use that to reach Sally?" he asked.

"Well, if it's true that most people hear conversations and see events through the WIIFM broadcast, then I think you might need to have a conversation with Sally about her frustrations and challenges, and see if it's possible to help her solve those by her changing—rather than everyone else changing."

Jack felt like a weight had been lifted from his shoulders. "Of course," he said to Sam.

Sam busied himself with the last items to be tidied in Jack's office.

"Thanks, Sam," Jack said. "I don't know how you got so wise, but I sure am thankful that you are here to share your insights with me."

"Oh, I'm not really that wise, I just like to watch people. People are quite predictable if you start paying attention to what they do."

The Approach

Jack had a meeting scheduled with Sally for ten. Normally, Sally would come to his office, but Jack had made sure that this particular meeting would take place in her office. He wanted her to be as relaxed as possible.

Jack knocked on Sally's door and saw her glance up. "Hey, Jack. Let me just finish this e-mail and I'll be right with you. Let's sit over there, okay?" Sally motioned to the small table with a number of chairs in the corner of her office.

Jack sat down and waited for a moment while Sally finished her e-mail. After a moment, she pushed back from her desk, grabbed a pen and a pad of paper, and came over to sit across from Jack at the table.

"Sorry," she remarked, "there always seems to be a crisis around here."

Jack smiled, "I understand, really I do. In fact, that was something that I wanted to speak with you about..."

Sally interrupted almost immediately, "Do you mind if we do some housekeeping first?"

She then launched into a list of problems that she was experiencing with the other department heads. Jack patiently took notes on the items that she brought up. When Sally finally seemed to be running out of feedback after about fifteen minutes, Jack promised to look into the items she had brought up.

"Okay. Your turn," said Sally.

Jack smiled to himself—an outside observer might have concluded that Sally was the boss based on who had controlled the focus of the meeting so far. But Jack was okay with that. He reminded himself that his purpose was to get Sally to be aware of the need for change in her interaction style, not to assert himself. That would only lead to outcomes that would not be helpful.

"I know you are aware that I have been spending some time with sales and customer service trying to help them implement some changes in the way that they are both handling the sales process and also how we work with our customers after the sale. While the results aren't yet where they need to be, they are absolutely moving in the right direction."

Jack paused to see what Sally's reaction would be. As it turned out, Sally didn't react much at all. She neither indicated agreement nor gave any sign that she disagreed. Jack took a deep breath. This was what was so hard in dealing with Sally. He never seemed to know what was happening or what would push her button until it was too late.

Jack decided to press forward. "I wanted to also talk with you about the groups that report up through you…"

Sally interrupted. "Look, Jack, I appreciate that you feel that this stuff can help in customer service and sales, but what we do here," she waved her arm to indicate the department, "it's different. We don't deal with the customer except maybe to resolve serious billing issues. I just don't see how the four faces stuff really applies around here."

That being said, Sally smiled and attempted to change the subject. "Now what I really could use some help from you on is the customer service group. They seem to think they have no responsibility to even attempt to collect what our customers owe us. For example—"

Jack cleared his throat and interrupted her. "Sally. While I realize you don't see the application for what we are doing in your groups, I'm asking you to stay with me here for a bit. If, at the end of this conversation, you feel that this won't help you, then I'll listen to whatever plans you have to help your groups run more effectively. Is that fair?"

Sally took a deep breath and reluctantly agreed.

Jack collected his thoughts for a moment and remembered what Sam had told him about What's In It For Me radio. He needed to get Sally to think about what she wanted to happen differently and how it would benefit her.

Jack began again. "I want you to think of your group two different ways. In fact, let's just think about finance for now."

Jack wrote "Finance" at the top of his notepad and then drew a line down the center of the page. On the left side he wrote "Inside" and on the right he wrote "Outside."

"I want you to think about the problems and challenges you experience from two perspectives. Inside refers to the problems and challenges that occur inside your group. Outside refers to the problems and challenges that occur outside your group that impact what happens in finance."

Jack paused. "Now which one is most natural for you to start on?"

Sally immediately said, "Outside."

Jack nodded. "While I know that would be the most natural place for most leaders to start, I have found that if we don't start on the inside, it is hard, if not impossible, to get the outside issues to go away."

Sally looked doubtful, but having agreed to hear him out, nodded her intent to play along.

Jack leaned into the table and asked the WIIFM question. "Sally, what are the challenges and frustrations inside the finance group that, if they went away, would make your life here more enjoyable?"

Sally sat back and thought for just a moment. "Jack, the stuff that frustrates me isn't what happens in here, it's what happens in other groups that ends up being a problem for us in finance."

Jack nodded. "I realize that; however, let's stay with inside first, even if it is a short list."

Jack waited patiently as Sally thought about his question. "Okay, it seems like people don't always take the initiative to get things done. They don't see the big picture. They seem to get more focused on the task than why it is important."

Having warmed up a bit, Sally started to get into the flow. "Urgency, or a lack of it, is a challenge too. People just don't seem to move fast enough. And I wish people would stay focused more on the job. Decision-making; I seem to have to make every decision around here. And, I don't know, I wish people were just a little more passionate about their work, you know, not just putting in time."

Jack took notes as Sally talked. When she was finished, he showed her his sheet.

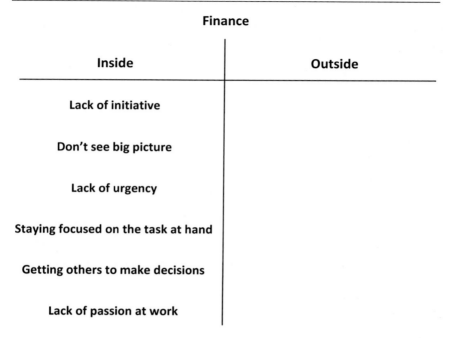

Finance

Inside	Outside
Lack of initiative	
Don't see big picture	
Lack of urgency	
Staying focused on the task at hand	
Getting others to make decisions	
Lack of passion at work	

Jack looked at Sally. "Anything else?"

"No, that's a fairly accurate list. I guess there were a few things I would like to change inside finance after all, but I still think the real issues are in the other departments," she added.

"I realize that, but hang with me here for a few more minutes. Would your quality of life here at work improve if these issues went away?"

"Well sure," said Sally, "but isn't that just the way things are? I mean, can any of that stuff really change?"

Jack noticed that the conversation was already getting to a better place. "Well, let's see, shall we? Let's take a look at this urgency challenge first, if that's okay with you. Tell me more about that."

Sally shrugged, "It's pretty simple, really. When there is a problem with, say, a client account, it needs to be addressed right away. When we delay calling the client, it doesn't make things better—it actually makes the client more frustrated and also delays how long it takes for us to collect what is owed."

"So what normally happens?" asked Jack.

"Well, at the start of every day I get a report of all client bills that are in dispute. It's normally a pretty long list. In order for it to get to that list, it has to have been referred to us by customer service and then my staff works on it as well, so the account is getting pretty old."

"So then what happens?" asked Jack.

"Well, then I call them and resolve the problem."

"I see," said Jack. "Sally, let me ask you a question aside from what you would like to see customer service do differently. What would you like to see happen when it arrives in finance?"

"That's easy. My people need to call the customer and make contact with them as soon as possible."

"And what do they normally do?" asked Jack.

"They e-mail the customer who then typically e-mails back and nothing gets resolved. These kinds of challenges need to be resolved with a conversation, not an e-mail."

"So why do you think they e-mail the customer rather than calling?" asked Jack.

"I think it's easier for them. I've asked them to call, but even if they do, it doesn't seem to lead to a resolution of the problem. It still ends up on my desk."

"So what do you do?" asked Jack.

"I call the customer and find out what happened. I review the file and make a determination of what we need to do to get the customer to pay what is fair."

Jack nodded. "But that all really should be done by your staff, right?"

"Or by the customer service department before it even gets to us."

Jack nodded. "Alright, but let's stay with your staff for now. Okay?"

Sally nodded. "Sorry," she said.

"Sally, what color did we say you were?"

Sally smiled. "I think I would be referred to as a 'flaming red.'"

Jack laughed, "Okay, so dealing with these types of disputes comes pretty naturally for you, right? I mean, you don't avoid difficult conversations, do you?"

"Of course not, that only makes things worse."

Jack nodded, "Sally—what do you think the behavioral style of many of your people would be?"

Jack pulled his guide out and let Sally take a look at it.

"Probably green or blue," Sally remarked. "Why?"

"Because, it has been my experience that dealing with conflict is more difficult for greens," said Jack.

"So I hired the wrong people?" asked Sally.

Jack responded quickly, "Not necessarily. Remember, behavioral style is just what you are comfortable doing, it doesn't mean you can't build skill in areas that are less comfortable for you."

"So greens are less comfortable with conflict, and may seek to avoid it. But they could build skill in dealing with conflict and become good at it?" asked Sally.

"Exactly," responded Jack. "They'll likely never be as comfortable with it as a red, but they can certainly be good at it. In some ways, because they are so good at understanding where others are coming from, they can even resolve issues that others may struggle with."

"So what do I need to do?"

"Well, have you ever considered coaching them on how to resolve these issues?"

"I've tried. They just don't get it."

Jack considered that and asked, "When you coach them, what does that look like?"

Sally shrugged. "I tell them to call the customer and ask why the bill is not paid."

"I think I understand. See, for you, Sally, this type of conversation is not really something you have to think about. It just happens. What you may need to do is slow down and map out all the different ways that the conversation could go and how you would like your rep to respond in those different situations. Also, you need to think about this like your people would. In other words, do not think, *How would I do this as a red?* but rather, *How would a green do this?*"

Sally nodded. "And then I train them on how to do it, right?"

"Exactly," smiled Jack.

Sally sat back and looked at Jack. "Okay, I'm going to try it your way."

Jack got up and smiled at Sally. "Can I check in tomorrow and see how it is going?" he asked.

"Sure," replied Sally.

CHAPTER TEN

Expecting the Unexpected

The next morning was a whirlwind for Jack, and it was not until later in the morning that he could make good on his commitment to touch base with Sally on what kind of progress she had made on her goals.

Jack was not sure what to expect as he made his way toward the finance department. He had come to realize that Sally, as a red, often came across as combative and obstinate. However, she was incredibly passionate and committed to whatever she set her mind to. The question that Jack was seeking an answer to was: How effective had he been at getting her to focus on how others on her team might perceive the direction and instruction she was delivering?

As Jack made his way into the finance department, he saw that Sally's door was wide open. As he walked across the main workspace that made up the finance department, he noticed that people were watching him progress toward Sally's office. As he knocked on the door, Sally looked up from the reports she was studying and walked around from behind her desk, which was new in and of itself, and welcomed him into the room with a broad smile.

Sally motioned to the small conference table as she greeted him and they both sat down. Jack had been prepared to discuss his previous conversation with her, and had in fact given a fair amount of thought as to the way he would approach the subject. But before he even had a chance to begin, Sally opened up the conversation.

"You know, Jack, I was pretty skeptical about this idea that perhaps by altering the way I was working with people that it would improve the way things ran around here. In fact, even during our conversation yesterday, I was pretty skeptical about the things you were saying. But the more we talked, the more I realized that perhaps even though I wasn't causing many of the problems, I wasn't doing anything to make them better, either."

Jack sat back in his chair and thought about Sally's comment for a moment. He said, "Sally, I think that's probably true. I think a lot of times as leaders we are not causing the problems, but it's our job to figure out what we need to do differently; and many times it seems unfair that we even have to deal with them at all."

Sally nodded as she looked back at Jack. "I told you yesterday I was going to give what you said a fair try, and I did do that. I actually sat down with people and started trying to think about the way they would deal with conflict with a client or a customer rather than the way I would do it. I think I've been doing this job for so long that perhaps I took for granted that people knew how to have difficult conversations with individuals. The more questions I asked of my staff, the more I realized that they were very nervous, not just about having the conversation, but about the fact that they would have to come to me and tell me if it didn't go well.

"So I started to do two things differently yesterday. The first thing is that, I started to ask more questions, and I've determined that almost everyone on my staff needs some training around how to have difficult conversations. That's something I would really like to talk to you about. The second thing I realized is I need to be less conflict oriented when people bring me challenges or frustrations or when they're having difficulty with something. I need to be more open to the fact that perhaps the way I respond to them causes them to be reluctant to come to me with their challenges."

Jack thought about Sally's comments and marveled at how far Sally had come in such a short period of time. He then reflected that Sally was a red and so often the things that we think of as people being difficult or people being obstinate are just a red's way of dealing with challenges and problems. They tend to hit them head on and to tell you exactly where they are coming from. The good thing about that, Jack realized, is that at least you know where they're coming from. The bad thing is that you have to work with them to make sure they understand there is a different way of interacting with people.

Jack was aware that as a red, Sally would be ready to move on and would not want to dwell on what had already happened, so he asked, "Well, Sally, what do you think you need to do next?"

Not surprisingly, Sally didn't have to think a long time to come up with an answer to that question. She said, "I've been giving that a lot of thought. I think if I can get people here in my department some training around conflict resolution and how to have difficult conversations, then people will be a whole lot more willing to talk to clients. There's another thing I've decided I need to do," and she smiled as she looked at Jack and said this, "because I'm a red I have a tendency to be less receptive to questions and tend to be curt and short with people. All that causes people to be a little less willing to come to me with challenges, so I need to slow down, I need to be more receptive, more open to people. Rather than automatically barking out an answer to a question because of my high sense of urgency, I need to ask people, 'Well, what do you think you need to do?'"

She pulled the report over from the corner of her desk. Jack recognized it as being the report that indicated the number of accounts and the amounts that were overdue from the customer base.

She said, "I've been looking at this and taking the responsibility for all of these accounts that are past due, and I've realized that it's really the account managers that really need to be working on that. I need to work with my people, and when someone is past due, I need to leave the responsibility with them to solve the problem rather than solving it for them."

Jack nodded his head. "Well, it sounds like you've got a good handle on what you need to do differently. And I want to commend you for the fact that you've made some changes so quickly and you are aware of some of the other changes you need to make."

Sally smiled as Jack got up, shook her hand and told her how pleased he was with the progress she had made and asked if it would be alright if he checked back with her in a couple of days. Sally said, "Sure, that would be fine."

As Jack left Sally's office, he thought back to how unfair his initial evaluation of Sally had been. He had thought that Sally perhaps might not make the cut, when in fact at least part of the problem was the way he had been interacting with her.

Last but Not Least

As Jack made his way towards his office, he decided that this probably was a good time to have his first conversation with Bob, so he changed direction and headed over to the IT department.

Bob, not surprisingly, was deeply involved in working his way through a spreadsheet when Jack knocked on his door. He was so involved in what he was doing that he did not even notice that Jack was standing at the door of his office until Jack had been there for a little bit. Jack lightly knocked on the door again. Bob looked up and politely asked Jack to come in. Jack sat down in front of his desk, and Bob waited for Jack to initiate the conversation.

Jack looked at him and said, "So, Bob, how are things going?"

Bob replied without any change of facial expression, "They're going well."

Jack smiled to himself. Bob's response could easily be construed to be unfriendly or uncommunicative. However, remembering that Bob was a blue, Jack was not surprised that Bob did not share a lot of information at this point. Jack mentally reviewed what he knew about the blue style. As he recalled, they preferred things to be more factual, more detailed, more planned out—and at a slower pace.

Jack asked, "How are things going between you and the sales team?"

Bob sat back in his chair and considered Jack's question.

"Well," Bob began slowly, "it's really too early to tell. However, the early indicators are positive. They seem to be making fewer concessions to prospective customers that are quite often either unnecessary, or at the very least, create a lot of extra work here that distracts us from making the progress we need to make on new product development."

"I know that has been frustrating for you and your team in the past," replied Jack.

Bob shifted his weight in his chair and furrowed his brow. "Yes, it has. I have to tell you, however, that I am concerned that they will be back to their old ways, and we will be back to chasing our tails."

Jack realized that the tendency to see what could go wrong was probably pretty common with the blue style. They often seemed to be planning for the worst. This made them very good at anticipating what might go wrong; however, it could also cause them to miss key opportunities when taken to the extreme.

"I think that is something that we need to guard against, and I would be interested in you letting me know if things start to slip back to the old way of doing things," Jack replied.

"Bob, I know you are aware that we have started to look at how we can use the four faces model to help each department run more smoothly, both internally and also with other departments. I wondered if you had given any thought to what challenges we might be able to work on with the IT department."

Bob seemed to ponder Jack's question for at least a full minute. "I wondered when you would get around to speaking with us in IT," began Bob.

Jack studied Bob's facial expressions as he began to speak. However, he could see no indication of whether Bob was amused, indifferent, or upset by the fact that his was the last department for Jack to address. Of course, Jack was getting used to not getting a lot of visual feedback from individuals with the blue behavioral orientation.

As Bob had not really posed the timing of his arrival as a question, but more as a statement, Jack decided to let Bob continue without addressing it directly.

Bob continued after a short pause. "I was thinking back to our conversation the first week you were here."

Bob pulled a typed sheet out of a file that he had sitting on his desk. Jack recognized it as the document that Bob had typed up for him during their initial discussion about challenges and frustrations.

Strengths:

- Skilled people that work hard

- Great technical skills

Opportunities:

- Need more people

Challenges and Frustrations:

- Need more people

- Unclear expectations as to what products are supposed to do

- Project parameters continually change causing delays

- Sales pushes too hard for product release before adequate testing has been done

Jack was struck once again by the level of detail and preparation that was evident with the blue style. He took a few moments to reread the document. He had learned over the last few months to slow down and be thorough when dealing with blues.

After he was finished reviewing the document, Jack nodded and asked Bob, "What would you change based on where we are today compared to that first week we spoke?"

"Well," began Bob, "I still believe we have great people that work hard and are technically skilled. I have, however, begun to reconsider whether we truly need more people. I'm not saying we don't, I just need some additional time for some of the changes that have occurred around here to filter through our workload. If sales continues to be more cooperative in terms of not promising customized features, then maybe we can remain at our current staffing levels. But that's a big 'if,'" he added with a wry smile.

Jack nodded his agreement and encouraged Bob to continue.

"As I consider the challenges I outlined earlier, I think that almost all of them are connected."

"What do you mean?" asked Jack.

"Well, one essentially leads to the other. It's a chain reaction." Bob took a pad of paper and sketched out what he was referring to:

Unclear expectations

$\downarrow$

Project parameters constantly change

$\downarrow$

We have inadequate time to test before product launch

"If we could gain more clarity on the front end of what we are supposed to be building, then I think there would be less changes required, and we would not be so behind schedule all the time."

Jack considered what Bob was suggesting. "So you believe that the root cause of many of the delays and also the quality issues with the products' releases stem from the way the projects are designed in the first place?" asked Jack.

"Yes, I do," replied Bob, showing more emotion than Jack had seen up until this point. "The problem is that Sally's R&D group and the sales team never seem to give us adequate direction and information at the start of a product development cycle. It seems to us like we are chasing a moving target all the way through the project."

"Do you think that it would be helpful to work with Sally and Carl on the way we scope out projects?" asked Jack.

"I think it is the only way we can make progress here," agreed Bob.

Jack contemplated what Bob was saying. "Alright, I can set that up," said Jack. "However, I have something for you to consider as we get ready for that meeting."

Jack paused and considered how to say what he wanted to say. "It has been my experience that there is almost always this type of tension between the user of IT systems and the people that design them."

"You're saying that you've seen this before, is that right?" asked Bob.

"Well, not exactly the same thing by any stretch. However, I have seen this sort of tension before."

"What did you do to solve the challenge?" asked Bob.

"I think what I have seen is that it is difficult for the users of IT systems to understand the complexity of what they are asking for."

"Amen to that!" replied Bob.

Jack smiled at Bob's outburst. "What I have seen is that although it is hard to get business people to 'speak IT,' it is much easier to get IT people to ask better questions so that they understand the purpose of the requests rather than reacting to them."

Bob thought about that for some time. "So you're saying that our IT people react in a very blue way, asking lots of questions about what the business wants, when we should be trying to find out why they want it?"

"Exactly," replied Jack. "You see, you guys are the experts at 'how' to get things done. What you need to know first is 'why' the business is asking for something."

"Because we may be able to deliver it in a more efficient manner," agreed Bob. "That's why they are always going on about us not seeing the big picture, isn't it?" asked Bob.

"Perhaps," conceded Jack. "We would have to ask them to be sure."

Bob thought about what Jack was proposing. "I think we need to teach our people the four faces model. Then they will be more open to learning how to speak the language that sales and R&D want to talk. It's going to take some work, though, to get them to think more like end users."

Jack nodded his agreement. "I'll set up a meeting with Sally and Carl so we can go over what we are proposing with them. We'll need them to be more aware of the challenges that we have discussed so that they can support you and your team in scoping projects more effectively."

"That would be great!" said Bob as he and Jack stood up and started toward the door. "You know, when we started this four faces stuff I really wasn't that bought in. But you know, I think a lot of the interpersonal conflict we experience both professionally and personally would improve if we spent a little more time trying to understand the perspective of other people. I may have actually applied this more at home with my son than I have at work up to this point. Things have gotten a lot better between us."

Bob didn't look like he wanted to elaborate further, so Jack did not press him on the subject. "Thanks, Bob. I'm excited about the opportunity to help you and your team make progress on the challenges we have discussed. But I am even more excited that this is helping you at home."

CHAPTER ELEVEN

Into the Details

Jack worked over the next few days to schedule the necessary meetings with Bob's staff to review the four faces model and go over how it would apply to working with the project teams, as well as how they might utilize it to work more effectively with each other. As Jack had suspected, there was a fair degree of anticipation to hear about the model and how they could use it within IT. Jack had been pleased that the success they had created some momentum as they moved to successive departments.

However, it was later in the week before Jack could follow through on his commitment to have a meeting with Bob, Sally, and Carl. Jack had decided to let Bob hold the project-planning meeting in the smaller conference room that was adjacent to the IT department. Sally and Carl arrived a few minutes early and were deep in conversation as they walked in. Unlike other conversations that he had observed between this pair, this one seemed to be almost cordial. Jack made a mental note to make sure that he spoke to them and reinforced this new way of working together.

They all settled in to the conference room, and Jack led off with an explanation of why he and Bob had wanted to meet.

"I wanted to meet with the three of you to see if we can come up with a better process for planning IT initiatives as we move forward."

Jack glanced over to Sally as he spoke and was pleased to see that she was not doing her usual eye rolling. "Bob and I have discussed the way things have been planned in the past, and he has agreed that it would be desirable to have his project planners work very hard to ask better questions of your teams, so that they can get a better sense of what business results the initiative is supposed to deliver."

Bob added, "I think we may have gotten caught up in the weeds a little too much, or at least we have gotten sucked into the details of the project a little too soon. We're going to be working with the IT team to ensure they understand that they must first understand the 'why' of the project, and only then will we try to figure out the 'what' and the 'how.' I think that if we do that, we can eliminate a lot of the rework and issues around the appearance that project parameters are shifting."

Jack watched Sally and Carl. Carl was nodding energetically and seemed to be in total approval of what had been presented thus far. Not surprisingly, Sally seemed to be reserving judgment.

Sally leaned forward and remarked, "That all sounds great, and I think that will be a big help. However, I think I would be correct in assuming that you did not invite us down here to just share that Bob's group is going to change the way they are working with us, did you? There must be something you need from us."

Sally's last sentence hung in the air—more of a statement and a challenge than a question.

Jack noticed that Carl's brow was now creased as he considered what Sally had said. He knew Sally had not meant to challenge him or Bob, it was just her natural way of interacting. He needed to be careful not to overreact to her statement, as he knew her intention was just to speed the meeting along, not to derail it. He also knew that without the four faces model, he might have reacted out of frustration, rather than understanding.

Bob looked over at Jack, clearly communicating that he would prefer Jack handle what needed to be said next.

"Well," began Jack, "Bob's people are going to be making a lot of changes in the way that they interact with your team on the project planning. However, we also need your support in getting your people on the project planning teams to work more effectively with the IT group."

Carl tilted his head to the side. "What do you need from us?" he asked. "We just tell them what we want."

Jack nodded his head. "Well, that's only part of the puzzle. You see, the IT team has to have clear project parameters, because if they don't, they will end up building a solution that is incomplete. What we need you both to do," he said, addressing Sally and Carl, "is make sure that you get your team to slow down and really think through their expectations prior to and during the project planning phase. I know both of you are more comfortable with things moving at a faster pace, but there is a lot of detail work accomplished in IT, and we owe it to them to make sure we give them adequate direction. That way, they can build the correct solution the first time around."

Sally cleared her throat. "While we may rush things sometimes, we don't have a crystal ball, Jack. I mean, there are times that we just don't anticipate a change in the business environment. Is IT going to be receptive to those changes, or are they going to hold us to the original projects specs?"

Jack decided to let Bob field this one. Bob considered Sally's question as he spun his pen on top of his pad of paper. "I think that if our people feel that they were given adequate direction out of the gate, then they will be mature enough to realize that business conditions fluctuate. It's when it is quite obvious that there was a lack of initial planning that is causing the project parameters to shift that they become frustrated."

Carl spoke up, "Well I for one don't see any problem with that. I mean, it won't be easy, but we can slow down and work through the details."

"As long as you can keep your people from getting stuck in the weeds," added Sally. "I mean, we can't design the specs with every contingency in mind," she added.

"I agree," said Bob. "Why don't the three of us monitor the progress we are making on this so that we can each keep our teams on the right track?"

Carl immediately nodded his head in agreement, while Sally reluctantly agreed.

As the meeting broke up, Jack made a point of walking out of the room toward the finance area so that he could chat with Sally for a few minutes.

"I noticed that you and Carl seemed to be getting along quite well as you walked into the meeting," he began.

Sally gave him a little smile. "Oh you noticed that, did you? Well, he's not all that bad if you can get past his sunny, 'everything is always great' demeanor. In fact, I probably could use a little more of that."

Jack stopped as they reached the entrance to the finance department. "Sally, I really appreciate the way you are working with the team and the changes you are making. Is there anything I can do to help you?"

Sally seemed to hesitate as she decided what to say. "Well, actually, I think things are going much better. Sales seems to be on the right track and the idea of not making all those customized allowances for clients seems to be paying off. We aren't bleeding red like we were. In fact, the changes made in sales are paying off in our retention numbers as well. And that is making our collection issues much more manageable as we are not dealing with as many customers that are putting their accounts into dispute. All in all, I think that I owe you an apology. It seems I was wrong about the direction you were taking. It has worked out pretty well."

Realizing that this was indeed high praise from a red, Jack smiled to himself.

Jack nodded as he responded, "Well, it is primarily due to a lot of hard work from a really talented team."

As Jack walked back to his office, he thought to himself that he hoped that Sally's assessment had not been premature. They were certainly not out of the woods yet.

CHAPTER TWELVE

Payoff

While the next few months were anything but a walk in the park for Jack and his team, the sales numbers continued to increase steadily month over month. But more importantly, the sales team became more focused on the right type of business. At first, Jack needed to be involved with Carl and his team, especially when the numbers started to look down in a particular month, as Carl would have a tendency to start making commitments and concessions that he was supposed to be staying away from.

However, as time went on, Jack sensed that Carl was becoming more comfortable with the sales process that had been set up, and was less likely to chase the wrong kind of business. Jack was also pleased that Carl was spending more time coaching his people and diving into what was getting in the way of them achieving their goals.

The changes in the sales group also had a positive impact on the customer service team. As the sales team started to pursue and close business without the promise of as much customization, John's team had been able to focus more diligently on learning and mastering the core of the company's product offerings. That had allowed the customer service reps to be more knowledgeable and helpful to the clients, reducing hold times and increasing customer satisfaction. In addition, employee satisfaction in the call group was at an all-time high.

Jack's suspicions about the customer service team being far too large for the size of AmeriSys had in fact borne out. As the company started to run more efficiently, Jack noticed that many of the customer service team started to voice concerns that their hard work might lead to a reduction in personnel, and that some people might lose their jobs. Jack and John had brainstormed different ways to address this challenge, looking for ways to redeploy talented employees to other parts of the company.

Jack knew that this type of exercise was uncomfortable for John but he also knew that he needed to make some tough choices about staffing. Ultimately, John had committed to reducing the head count on his team by about a third. Fortunately, Carl had been able to absorb a number of John's team into the sales group, and Sally had been able to work with a number of others and move them into the finance and administration group. Between those moves and the normal attrition that had occurred, John had been able to get close to his target head count. In fact, had the work environment not improved as much as it had over the past months, they would have had more people leaving, and they would have needed to start hiring. Jack had no intention of laying off anyone in the group in order to get to the exact number they had agreed on. In fact, he anticipated that they would need to start hiring for John's group within a few months as the sales numbers continued to increase.

Sally had been Jack's biggest surprise. Her initial combativeness, with both himself and everyone else, had not necessarily gone away; it was just more muted. She seemed to be more aware of how she was perceived by others and when her direct and assertive behavior may have become counterproductive.

In fact, Jack was pleased that she may have become his most ardent supporter. He had heard through the grapevine that she had taken to task some of the more aggressive board members when they had been trying to elicit information from her about why the company was not moving more aggressively on new markets that had been identified. Jack thought, not for the first time, that his initial assessment of her had been wrong. His perceptions of her had been colored by his bias, and he felt a great deal of gratitude that Sam had taken the time to share with him his insights on the four faces.

Sally's department had made great strides in employee engagement, and Jack felt like there was a real sense of ownership that could only be seen as an endorsement of Sally's desire to collaborate with them and hold them accountable for their work product, rather than taking control when things were not going as expected.

The IT team had also made amazing progress. Of course, it was not all positive. There was still the usual friction between the project planning team and the developers. However, the reduction in customized work coming out of the sales team had allowed Bob's group to focus more on ensuring that project parameters were better identified and documented. They had become quite skilled at asking the right questions and drilling down into the *why* of requested product features, rather than getting *stuck in the weeds,* as Sally liked to call it.

All of this had a positive impact of the launch of new products, as there was more time to ensure that product launches were tested adequately. The last major revision to one of the core products had significantly fewer bugs that needed to be fixed, and most of them had been identified before the target launch date. All of this led to fewer customer service calls to fix problems, and therefore to higher retention rates within the customer base.

All in all, Jack felt like AmeriSys was on its best footing in a number of years.

He still, however, had a nagging feeling of doubt as he approached his first anniversary as CEO. As it turned out, there was a full board meeting just three days after his one-year anniversary. Jack had planned his presentation of the company's results to date with painstaking detail and had also included his projections for the next twelve months.

The morning of the board meeting, Jack arrived early and found Sam making his usual rounds in the lobby area.

"Hey there, Sam," he called as he entered the building.

Sam looked up from his duties and smiled broadly at Jack. "Hello back at you. Are you ready for the big meeting today?"

Jack had long ago stopped being surprised by Sam's almost uncanny ability to know everything that was happening at AmeriSys. He smiled to himself and answered, "Ready as I will ever be." Then he added, "On a more serious note, I wanted to thank you for all the insight and advice that I have received from you over the past year. I am not sure that I would be standing here today if it was not for you."

"Don't be silly," replied Sam as he emptied a garbage can. "You would have gotten here with or without me."

"No, I don't think so, Sam. You see, I made a commitment to my wife when things were really at a low point that I would leave this job rather than have it ruin our home life. So, while I might have been able to accomplish this without your help, it would have taken a lot longer, and I really don't think I would have stuck it out. So, I'll say it again. Thank you."

This time Sam only smiled.

They continued the friendly banter that Jack had come to value so much for some time, until some of the other employees started to arrive.

"Look at the time!" remarked Sam. "I better get busy or there will be heck to pay with the big boss."

Jack smiled as he crossed the lobby area and climbed the stairs to the next floor.

Sam sure was a rare bird. No, *unique* would be a better word to describe him.

Jack's morning almost flew by. It was eleven o'clock before he knew it, and he took a deep breath as entered the boardroom to meet with the full board.

The sun was shining through the windows as he walked in. "Greetings, everyone," he began...

NEXT STEPS

To receive a complimentary overview of how to utilize the Four Faces Model in your organization to:

- Increase sales
- Increase customer retention and create WOW!
- Increase leadership effectiveness
- Increase teamwork and communication
- Increase productivity

go to:

www.transformingresults.com/fourfacesmodel

ABOUT THE AUTHOR

Andrew Oxley is an internationally recognized speaker, consultant, and author. He is the president of The Oxley Group, a highly successful training and consulting firm with a focus on bottom line results. He gives over a hundred presentations a year on leadership, customer service, teamwork, and productivity.

Andrew lives near Atlanta, Georgia, with his wife and four children. You can reach him at The Oxley Group's website, www.transformingresults.com, or at aoxley@transformingresults.com.